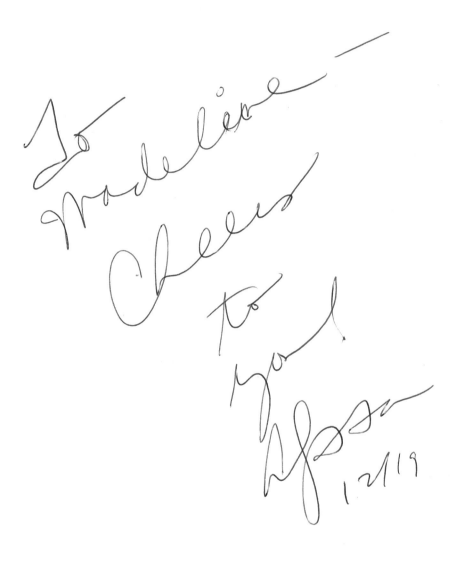

To Madeleine —

Cheers

to you!

ADDITIONAL PRAISE FOR *LEADERSHIP & LIFE HACKS*

"Like Alyssa herself, *Leadership & Life Hacks* is upbeat, can-do, and energizing. It is a great resource for women at all points in their career."

—**Marjorie Benton**, *founder, Chicago Foundation for Women; former chair, Save the Children; former US ambassador to UNICEF; board member, Benton Foundation, Partners in Health in Haiti, Bulletin of Atomic Scientists*

"Alyssa is an all-star educator, an all-star leader and civic activist, and an equally all-star friend—a true triple threat. She is a master storyteller and powerful communicator. I am so delighted that her unique talent, previously directed at her organizations and some of the world's finest MBA students, is now available more broadly via *Leadership & Life Hacks.*"

—**Wendy Berger**, *board member, Green Thumb Industries; CEO and president, WBS Equities, LLC*

"*Leadership & Life Hacks* is a perfect reflection of its author's intellectual agility and commitment to being a lifelong learner. I can't imagine anyone not both enjoying and benefiting from its useful stories and suggestions about making your life more efficient and impactful."

—**Christie Hefner**, *former chairman, CEO, Playboy Enterprises; strategic advisor and progressive activist*

"Flew through *Leadership & Life Hacks* and immediately gave it to my daughter, as we both needed to read it."

—**Jim Karas**, *#1* New York Times *best-selling author and entrepreneur*

"Since I met Alyssa at college, I have marveled at her ability to squeeze the very most out of life. I am thrilled to have this enumerated list of just how she does it! As an overwhelmed working mom desperately searching for consistency and efficiency, I cannot wait to put these life hacks into action."

—**Kellie Martin**, *actor, director, producer, and friend of the author*

"Alyssa has been a dear friend for over fifteen years, and through our marriages, children, health challenges, career setbacks, and triumphs we have learned together that success is not about the elusive work-life balance but instead focused on integration. Surround yourself with those who share your values and push you to be better. Alyssa has played that role for me, and I look forward to our next combination ladies' brunch, kids' playdate strategy session."

—**Emily Melton**, *managing partner and cofounder, Threshold Ventures*

"I've watched Alyssa develop and hone these hacks since we were kids. Learning from her ability to bet on herself and those around her has influenced how I deal with friends, family, and even with my team in the operating room. Share in her contagious energy and determination by reading this book!"

—**Amanda Munoz**, *otolaryngologist, head and neck surgeon, and clinical assistant professor, Stanford Otolaryngology*

"Alyssa tells her story, showcasing her focus, energy, and talents. She has the exuberance and vision to lead companies while embracing family life and community responsibilities. Alyssa is a force making an impact!"

—**Cherilyn G. Murer**, *author and president of CGM Advisory Group; board member, Surgical Solutions*

"Alyssa is high-octane energy and smarts. Her professional range is enormous. It is highly unusual to succeed in both start-up and middle-market CEO capacities across different industries. Her warm and direct demeanor is genuine and refreshing. Effective people follow, like, and respect her. Can't wait to see what she does next."

—**Greg Purcell**, *CEO, Arbor Investments*

Alyssa Rapp is a triple threat of talent, drive, and connectedness. This inspirational book puts together her life story and the lessons she has learned in a format that is relatable to every leader, wherever they are in their journey. Her life hacks are simple and impactful. You won't find them taught in an MBA program, but I expect you'll reach back and read them over and over again.

—**Madhav Rajan**, *Dean, University of Chicago Booth School of Business; George Pratt Shultz Professor of Accounting, University of Chicago Booth School of Business*

"My sister Alyssa has always impressed me with her drive and her boundless energy, and here she has shared some essential insights into living a successful and fulfilled—and fulfilling—life. What I'm most proud of, and what is delightfully on display here, is that she infuses all of her work in her job and her home life with a tremendous amount of heart."

—**Anthony Rapp**, *actor, singer, author's brother*

"As Alyssa goes, no wake-up call is necessary. Her discipline wakes her up. Her dedication is the fire that burns within. Her passion is her motivation."

—**Abdul Sillah**, *performance coach to Naomi Osaka and an array of the world's finest athletes*

"Alyssa is the next generation of leadership. She embodies the old-school values of a strong work ethic, thoughtful intellect, and deep compassion for others—just like her mother, Ambassador Fay Hartog-Levin. Whatever chapter of your life, *Leadership & Life Hacks* will help you make an impact."

—**Deirdre Joy Smith**, *founder and CEO, POWER: Opening Doors for Women*°

LEADERSHIP & LIFE HACKS

ALYSSA RAPP

LEADERSHIP & LIFE HACKS

INSIGHTS FROM A MOM, WIFE, ENTREPRENEUR & EXECUTIVE

100 Tips
for Achieving Your Goals
with Maximum Efficiency
and Impact

ForbesBooks

Published by ForbesBooks, Charleston, South Carolina.
Member of Advantage Media Group.

ForbesBooks is a registered trademark, and the ForbesBooks colophon is a trademark of Forbes Media, LLC.

Printed in the United States of America.

10 9 8 7 6 5 4 3 2 1

ISBN: 978-1-946633-83-5
LCCN: 2019914066

Cover design by Carly Blake.
Cover Photo by Robin Subar Photography.
Layout design by Megan Elger.

This publication is designed to provide accurate and authoritative information in regard to the subject matter covered. It is sold with the understanding that the publisher is not engaged in rendering legal, accounting, or other professional services. If legal advice or other expert assistance is required, the services of a competent professional person should be sought.

Advantage Media Group is proud to be a part of the Tree Neutral® program. Tree Neutral offsets the number of trees consumed in the production and printing of this book by taking proactive steps such as planting trees in direct proportion to the number of trees used to print books. To learn more about Tree Neutral, please visit **www.treeneutral.com**.

Since 1917, the Forbes mission has remained constant. Global Champions of Entrepreneurial Capitalism. ForbesBooks exists to further that aim by bringing the Stories, Passion, and Knowledge of top thought leaders to the forefront. ForbesBooks brings you The Best in Business. To be considered for publication, please visit **www.forbesbooks.com**.

To my mother: You are the consummate example of leading a life of impact. I could not have asked for a better mentor in this journey. Thank you for your tough love, unflinching support, and awesome role modeling. I can only imagine what the world would be if all children had mothers as fierce, intellectual, supportive, and brave as you. Thank you for all that you do for me and our family. I love you.

To my Hal: Thank you for your love, confidence, and support of the episodic versus daily balance in our lives. I am truly grateful to be your wife. Thank you for holding me tightly when the going gets tough and for always reminding me to keep swinging. I love you.

To our Audrey and Henriette: You are the lights of our lives. The reason to live life as efficiently as possible is to get every possible minute with you. The reason to live a life of impact is to help shape the best world possible for you.

I love you to the moon and back, forever and ever, always.

CONTENTS

ACKNOWLEDGMENTS

This book would not have been possible without ForbesBooks, first and foremost, and the vision of Adele Cisco on the ForbesBooks | Advantage Media team. Thank you for recruiting me so warmly and working with me so creatively.

I owe a major debt of gratitude to Bree Barton. Her compassion, brilliance as a writer, warmth as a human being, and passion for this project helped bring it to life as much as my own. From helping to architect the table of contents to helping shape the contents thereafter, *Leadership & Life Hacks* would not have been as fun to bring to life— or as efficient—without our live marathon content-generation sessions in Los Angeles, Chicago, Palo Alto, and San Diego. If a book two is to happen, I wouldn't consider doing it without you. *Thank you.*

A WORD FROM THE AUTHOR

Hack *(verb)*

1. cut with rough or heavy blows.
2. an act of computer hacking.

The dictionary defines "hack" as the use of a cutting instrument or a tool for good (hacking off dead branches) or evil (hacking your computer).

For the purposes of *Leadership & Life Hacks: Insights from a Mom, Wife, Entrepreneur & Executive,* I offer an alternate view. For the next 187 pages, "hacks" should be thought of as shortcuts, work-arounds, or work-throughs. Each chapter's hacks are summarized up front, in case all you have time for are the hacks themselves and not the narratives behind them. One must practice what one preaches …

You are welcome to read this book in any order: in sequence, out of sequence, or just by grabbing the chapter that is relevant to you today. Perhaps tomorrow, you'll find another relevant to your parent, sibling, best friend, life partner, business partner, or you again.

No matter how you read this book, I'm hoping at least one of these one hundred *Leadership & Life Hacks* proves as helpful to you in driving greater efficiency and impact in your life as they do in mine.

FOREWORD

My friend Alyssa Rapp is a force of nature. Smart, savvy, fierce, loyal. She knows what she wants out of life, isn't afraid to be honest and vocal about it, and will go after what she wants with all of her gusto. She has many great stories to tell and a ton of useful "hacks" as she calls them. I'm delighted that she is sharing her experience and insights broadly through this book.

I've had the benefit of being her friend and learning from her over the past decade. We've lived a few blocks from each other, become mothers at the same time, sent our children to the same school, and celebrated dozens of life milestones together—our engagements, weddings, and birthdays, big and small. We've turned to each other for advice during critical moments in motherhood and in our careers.

In modern storytelling, one-dimensional female characters are everywhere, creating the sense that women can't be two seemingly opposite things at once. Are you efficient or nurturing? Honest or nice? A leader or a helper? Career- or family-minded? These false dichotomies do a disservice to women by presenting these traits as binary choices. They aren't. In fact, in many cases, they actually represent positively correlated traits. You have more time to be nurturing if you are efficient. You can always deliver an honest message with kindness. A leader's role is, by definition, to support the team. Career experience often yields the creative inspiration that gives rise to better parenting.

Leadership & Life Hacks squares the circle, offering a hundred tips for turning these contradictions and complexities into rich, multi-dimensional advantages.

Alyssa herself is a complex, refreshing blend of traits: blunt but polite, funny yet serious, tough *and* nurturing. She defies stereotype and refuses to be categorized. I've learned so much from her and her tenacity that I'm sure you will too.

—**Marissa Mayer**, CEO and Cofounder of Lumi Labs; formerly the CEO of Yahoo and VP of Search and User Experience at Google; devoted wife and mother of three

NOW WHAT?

This book began the way most books begin: with a question.

The question came over a year and a half ago, shortly after my family moved back to Chicago. To understand *why* I asked the question—and all the circumstances that led me to it—we have to go back a little further.

Before the Chicago move, I'd spent the last twelve years in Silicon Valley. As an MBA student at Stanford, I fell in love with my first entrepreneurial idea—and also with my husband. Hal and I married and had two children, and for the better part of a decade, we split our time between Silicon Valley and the Midwest. During that decade I founded my first company, Bottlenotes, Inc., which started as an e-commerce play that shifted to become a leading digital media company in the US wine industry when a regulatory change by the California Alcohol Bureau of Control forced us to either raise a white flag or pivot. For better and for worse, I rarely quit. Which left us no choice but to pivot.

As both my professional and personal lives became more demanding, I was constantly renegotiating the work-family balance. The day our first daughter, Audrey, was born, I closed a crucial investor while driving to the hospital. I was literally signing in for the C-section when Husband Hal said to me, "It's time to shut it [the phone] down, Rapp. Time to have a baby."

By the time our second daughter, Henriette, was born two and a half years later, I was ready for a slight change. I would still work my tail off—as a childhood athlete, first a competitive gymnast and then a contemporary dancer; I don't know any other way—but I needed more flexibility and more freedom, and I wanted more time with my husband and daughters.

I started looking for ways to "hack the system" as a mom, wife, entrepreneur, and executive.

I started looking for ways to "hack the system" as a mom, wife, entrepreneur, and executive. By *hack*, I mean I was seeking high-impact strategies that would help me work more efficiently, achieve better outcomes, and more successfully balance my personal and professional lives.

I didn't know it then, but I was uncovering the very hacks you're about to read.

SAYING YES

After Bottlenotes exited to a hedge fund in 2015, I chose to take a couple of years as an advisor/consultant and lecturer in management at Stanford's Graduate School of Business versus jumping immediately back into the CEO seat.

I started AJR Ventures, a strategic advisory firm that served two family offices and two private-equity firms in Chicago and the Bay Area. I quickly discovered that I enjoyed working with private-equity firms more than venture capitalists as an operator. Private equity is purely driven by economic returns, making it more egalitarian, more objective, and less sexist, and thus more appealing to me.

Sometimes circumstances nudge us in certain directions or even expedite the timeline of major life decisions. In 2017 Hal's father passed away unexpectedly. We made the choice to move back to Chicago to be closer to his mom and also to my parents. It happened fast: I closed on a house in July, and we moved in August. By September our youngest daughter was two and a half and heading to preschool, and our oldest was starting kindergarten. I was ready to be a CEO again.

I knew that I didn't want to create something from scratch at that moment. A start-up is like a baby, and I already had two human babies—I wasn't ready for a third. As I thought about how to transition back to CEO life, I started having conversations with several private-equity firms in Chicago. Rather than boiling the ocean and doing a big, exhaustive search, talking to everyone, I let the process evolve more organically.

That's how I ended up in a conversation with Steven Taslitz, the chairman of Sterling Partners. Steven had founded companies *and* a PE firm, and I liked his entrepreneurial approach to private equity. I knew I wanted to run something that wasn't a start-up; I was most interested in running a company with a "running start" of $20–$50 million in topline revenue.

I liked Steven. He talked a lot about his daughters, and he clearly adores his wife. He wanted to meet my husband and wanted us to meet his family too. It felt like we were getting to know each other as people, not just potential business partners. He invited me to several diligence meetings at Sterling as a way for us both to see the other in action.

My favorite meetings that fall were those that I sat in on for a potential coffee deal that they ended up investing in (and that I anticipate you'll be hearing about on the NYSE or as a major M&A target in the future). From those meetings, we determined there was likely a good fit between Alyssa Rapp, Steven Taslitz, and Sterling Partners. The question became this: Which would be the right company to lead?

In the fall of 2017, Steven came to me with an idea. They had a portfolio company that needed a turnaround CEO, and it checked the box on size. Even better, it was fifteen minutes from my house. When not traveling for work, I'd be able to drop my girls at school—which is of absolute importance to me—be home by dinner, and log on later at night.

"The only catch," Steven said, "is that it's a B2B play—not B2C—and it's not consumer products or consumer internet but health care."

To which I replied, "Thanks so much, but I'm not sure."

At face value, Surgical Solutions was not the company most would have anticipated I would lead next, including me. I'd spent over a decade building consumer brands in Silicon Valley, followed by two years advising private-equity firms and family offices on consumer/luxury/e-commerce strategies and technology enablement. The class I created at Stanford's Graduate School of Business is entitled Dynamics of the Global Wine Industry. Up to that point, I had frankly been a Valley Girl—Silicon Valley and Napa Valley—and a consumer-product-focused and consumer-internet-focused one at that.

The more I thought about the opportunity at Surgical Solutions, the more it compelled me. I liked the idea of learning a new industry. I liked the idea of a double bottom-line benefit, meaning working in an industry that is improving lives—in Surgical's case, the satisfaction of health care providers—and hospitals' bottom lines, thus potentially improving patient outcomes. I liked the idea that by entering the health care industry, I'd be diving headfirst into an increasingly crucial and complex pillar of our national economy, one with skyrocketing costs (estimated by some to be 18 percent of our national GDP and growing[1]). These insights would continue to inform my career and civic engagement.

I had come from an industry mired in a quagmire of regulation, and I spent a decade mastering it, so highly regulated industries didn't intimidate me—in fact, if you carve out a niche in one, your position is all the more defensible. Here's the thing about an industry that's rife with regulation and inefficiency: it's also ripe for disruption.

That's not to say my decision to take the helm at Surgical was easy. I did my homework. I talked to

Here's the thing about an industry that's rife with regulation and inefficiency: it's also ripe for disruption.

three of the board members, including Kim Vendor Moffat, who was a talented friend of mine from high school. Kim had been at Sterling Partners for almost two decades, had been on the Surgical deal team, and had greatly influenced my decision to join the company via her transparency about its operations (good, bad, ugly) during her tenure on the board. She didn't paint a perfect picture, but she clearly laid out the challenges and the opportunity. Transparency—or radical honesty, as some are calling it these days—inspires confidence and builds trust.

---

1   John Commins, "Healthcare Spending at 20% of GDP? That's an Economy-Wide Problem," HealthLeaders, accessed August 19, 2019, https://www.healthleaders-media.com/finance/healthcare-spending-20-gdp-thats-economy-wide-problem.

I had a similar conversation with Surgical Solutions' board chair, Ancelmo Lopes, a veteran health care industry leader, executive, advisor, and board member, with whom I quickly gleaned I could have a relationship based upon easy, direct, and effective communication, which I knew would be crucial to my potential success. The same went for Jay Istvan, CEO of Suture Express, who added the additional benefit of also currently sitting in a CEO chair of a larger company in the health care space and providing the guidance and unique perspective to the table as such.

Lastly, I shared with Ancelmo and Steven that I would be interested in bringing on another board member: a woman. They kept true to their word, and within a month, Sterling had appointed the indomitable health care policy wizard Cherilyn Murer to Surgical's board at my initial urging.

Bottom line: they believed Surgical Solutions needed a good old-fashioned leadership reboot to get the job done. I wanted to test that thesis for myself too.

At Stanford we were trained that tried-and-true leadership is transferable across sectors and frankly transcends industry. I teach some of these principles today. So did I have what it took to lead the turnaround of a company in an industry that was brand new to me, based in a different town from where I ran my first company, and help shepherd an era of growth that would ultimately yield Sterling Partners the greatest possible return on its investment?

I knew Surgical wasn't a billion-dollar company. It was still young and nimble, roughly two hundred employees—by no means too big to fail. The job was to come in and scale revenue to $100 million as quickly as possible.

So I said yes.

Yes to a CEO job in an industry I knew nothing about. Yes to a city I had yet to live in full time as a wife, mom, entrepreneur, or executive. I knew it would be hard, challenging, sometimes scary. C'est la vie. Nothing ventured, nothing gained.

That's when I asked myself the question. The question that launched not just the next part of my career, but the process that would inevitably lead me here, writing this book. Two little words that catalyzed everything that came next.

So I said yes. Yes to a CEO job in an industry I knew nothing about. Yes to a city I had yet to live in full time as a wife, mom, entrepreneur, or executive.

Now what?

As I asked myself this question—this book was born.

LIFTING THE LID

After I said yes to Surgical, I spent the next three weeks talking to people internally and externally. I knew I wanted to show up on day one with the equivalent of what in the political world would be a one-hundred-day plan.

There's a saying in business school that while you're a student, anyone will take your call. When you're not a student, you're just another alum in the workplace, either a competitor or potential colleague. For the three and a half weeks after I accepted the CEO job—but before I officially stepped into the role—everyone was happy to contribute his or her perspective.

In a healthy but somewhat intimidating way, it made me realize how much I didn't know. Because I was hungry for wisdom, I reached out to my friend Jaime Irick, a West Point and Harvard Business

School alum who at the time was the CEO of Life Fitness. I asked him for a recommended reading list, and I read every book Jamie suggested (check out the appendix if you'd like to read these titles yourself). I had been assessed for the CEO role by ghSMART, where Andre Zafrani, now founder of Apogee Advisors, was unbelievably kind and gracious in giving me time-tested advice on how to attack the first quarter on the job.

What I had a harder time finding were books that spoke to being a successful businesswoman in concert with the many other roles I play. I'm not just a CEO—I am also a wife, mother, teacher, friend, athlete, board member, donor, and active political citizen.

I started asking more questions. Were there ways to be a committed and devoted wife, a loving and attentive mother, *and* a dedicated and hardworking CEO? What did success look like across the board? How could I reorganize my life to be even more effective personally and professionally in the upcoming one-to-two-year period?

The debate as to whether women can "have it all" has become a trite cliché. I won't be posing that question in these pages. Instead, *Leadership & Life Hacks* offers a behind-the-scenes look at my life in a Silicon Valley start-up, the private-equity world, the mom world, and all the other spaces I inhabit.

I'll take you with me into the boardroom and into my own home. We'll get granular (e.g., the power of personalized thank-you notes, why you should take board members to rock concerts), and we'll also ask big-picture questions. How do you manage an effective board meeting? How do you manage a household? What are some strategies for answering emails, staying fit, and best utilizing your time?

Many of my nearest and dearest female friends are powerful women in their industries—while also attempting to balance families and homes—and all are universally slammed. We're always seeking tangible ways to create more impact and efficiency in our lives. You might call them secret sauces or shortcuts to success. For the purposes of this discussion, let's call them hacks.

The hacks in this book are divided into two overarching sections: lead and live. Of course, for many of us, the two often blend together. I suggest you read *Leadership & Life Hacks* in whatever way feels most intuitive: front to back, back to front, or by cherry-picking chapters that resonate. There's no right or wrong approach.

I'm also a big believer in the power of story. To that end, each chapter of *Leadership & Life Hacks* is structured around a significant narrative (or narratives) from my life. Though the main events of the first four chapters happen to be in chronological order, I'll also be moving fluidly between different time periods. You'll find anecdotes from my childhood all the way up to my fortieth birthday party—and you'll see I've bullet-pointed all the hacks at the beginning of each chapter.

The content and concepts in this book can be applied to a wide variety of situations. My hope is that, whether you're a CEO, entrepreneur, businessperson, athlete, teacher, spouse, stay-at-home parent, community leader—even if you don't yet know exactly what you want to do—there are leadership and life hacks in these pages that will be useful to you.

My big goal in *Leadership & Life Hacks* is to inspire and demystify. I'll share simple tips and strategies that have worked for me—and I'll be unflinchingly honest about those that haven't. I've achieved modest success in my life, but that doesn't mean I've hit all singles and doubles.

The truth is, no matter how you define success, for the majority of successful people, it rarely comes as a home run. It's an ongoing treadmill of hard work, nimbleness, flexibility—and an openness to what you could always be doing better.

At the end of the day, to provide maximum impact in everything you do, as efficiently as possible, there's a whole level of orchestration behind the scenes of *how* you do it that no one ever sees.

PART ONE: LEAD

There will be hurdles to overcome. There will be plenty of nonbelievers and there will be abundant mistakes. But with hard work, there is no limit to what you can do.

—Abdul Sillah, Performance Coach to Naomi Osaka and an array of the world's finest athletes

There's no elevator to success. Everyone's gotta take the stairs.

—Alex Toussaint, Peloton

CHAPTER 1

ROMANCING THE CONSUMER: THE STORY OF BOTTLENOTES

Hacks 1–8, Summarized

LEADERSHIP HACK 1

Always focus on building a company that is built to last, not built to flip. Ironically, if you focus on selling your business, you're less likely to grow it into something that people will want to buy. But if you focus on building something enduring, that will ultimately help it get sold.

LEADERSHIP HACK 2

If you have a passion for something, educate yourself about the industry. Then ask what isn't working—and come up with a solution. It was only once I started reading up on New Vine Logistics and Wineshopper.com that I saw opportunity. No matter what field you're in, look for gaps or holes. Once you've sourced potential problems, you can create potential solutions.

LEADERSHIP HACK 3

If you're launching a consumer product start-up, look for ways to defray the inventory carrying cost. When you're a young company, you don't always have a lot of resources to play with. If you can look for ways to pare down on carrying costs (or even better, eliminate them entirely), you will be able to grow more quickly and efficiently.

LEADERSHIP HACK 4

Use technology to match people to products. We took a product that can feel esoteric and opaque and used the internet to bring the right wine to the right customers in a simple, efficient way. You can do this with any product or service. And if the technology doesn't exist, invent it, or partner with someone who can.

LEADERSHIP HACK 5

Romance your customers. The digital age hasn't diminished the need for developing close relationships with your customers—if anything, it's made it all the more important. Personal touches still matter. Whatever you're selling, treat it as more than just a transaction.

LEADERSHIP HACK 6

Think outside of the box to get more eyes and hands on your product. You don't always need money to execute smart marketing for your business. Creativity can transcend dollars. When a PR agency asked me for thousands of dollars, I countered with thousands of dollars of wine and in-kind wine club memberships—and probably galvanized even more customers that way.

LEADERSHIP HACK 7

If someone thought of an idea first, don't be too proud to personalize the concept and use it again. We riffed off the RedEnvelope theme at Bottlenotes with signature blue envelopes, but there are countless ways you can take an existing concept and innovate on it. You don't want to plagiarize or get into trouble with copyright, of course, but as the saying goes, "Nothing new under the sun." Take good ideas and refurbish them, adding your own unique, irresistible twist.

LEADERSHIP HACK 8

Leverage the power of alignment. It doesn't have to be celebrity endorsements (though those are always great). Find people or brands with a broader reach than yours or people or brands who are aligned with your mission, and get them excited about what you're offering. In today's world, this includes influencer and micro-influencer marketing. You'll gain the halo effect of the brand affinity, and they'll ultimately help proselytize for you.

* * *

For many twentysomethings, the postcollege years can be a time of wondering and wandering in existential uncertainty.

I was not one of those people. I enrolled at Stanford Business School with the express goal of becoming an entrepreneur. Before long, the seeds of various ideas began to germinate.

At Yale I'd fallen in love with art history. Studying the history of art served as a window into people, culture, history, and politics for me in a colorful and provocative way. Upon graduation, I missed this role that art history served in my life—and the "study" of wine became its substitute. Like art, wine offered a window into culture, history, and politics, in addition to cuisine and world travel.

Once at graduate school at Stanford, I researched a supply chain management firm in the US wine industry that later turned into an academic case study on said firm that I wrote in partnership with my supply chain management professor. I pursued a summer internship working for a classmate's father's boutique import company of New Zealand wines (that classmate's father later became my first investor). And I joined the leadership team of the GSB's Wine Circle, a student-run entity that provided professionally led educational wine events to our membership on an almost weekly basis.

When copresiding over the GSB Wine Circle, I noticed something interesting that served as a seedling for a business idea. During our events, when we tasted wine together, members were thirsty for not just more wine, but for more wine *knowledge*. We *wanted* to learn about wine, and even better, established wineries were willing to teach us. I was astounded that industry icons and Stanford GSB alums like Jack Cakebread of Cakebread Cellars and Peter Mondavi Jr. of Charles Krug Winery were eager to educate and potentially recruit the next generation of wine enthusiasts. Was there a business model to be had that helped wine brands access the next-generation wine enthusiast, particularly one that leveraged internet personalization trends of the day to do so? And that allowed wine enthusiasts to receive ongoing education on which wines were most right for them?

THE AMERICAN DREAM

At twenty-four, I never doubted I could start my own company. I credit two people for the inspiration, arguably the two most important Jewish elders in my life: my grandfather and my stepfather.

My maternal grandparents were prominent Jews who left the Netherlands in the midst of World War II to escape the Holocaust.

Having returned to their home in The Hague after the war, they realized so many of their friends and family had perished that it was time to start anew in the United States. Thus my mother's parents emigrated from Holland to the United States in 1948; my mother was the first of their children to be born in the States in 1948, their first three having been born in the Netherlands and Suriname.

My *opa*—Dutch for *grandfather*—sold stationery and print supplies door to door after arriving in the States. After about a year, he said to himself, "There is a more efficient way to do this business," having been raised in a family that owned a paper business in The Hague. He bought a printing company in New York City called Downs Printing. Later in the 1950s, he took a turboprop plane to Puerto Rico to explore and ultimately buy the factory where artist brushes were made. He expanded the business to include makeup brushes, becoming the first to make "blush on" brushes for Revlon. In the 1960s, they sold the Delta Brush Company to Binney & Smith (makers of Crayola), likely around the time that my *oma* (my maternal grandmother) became terminally ill with cancer. My opa invested the proceeds of the sale of the packaging company into what by present-day terms would have been a tech start-up—a company called IBM, which he had been investing in since the 1950s.

Opa spent his "third act" of life traveling extensively with his second wife, having lost his first wife to ovarian cancer at age fifty. He returned to Europe each winter in their home in Cap d'Antibes and took frequent trips to visit his children: my eldest aunt and her family in Ohio and eventually Connecticut, my second aunt and her family in Holland, my mom and us in Chicago, and my uncle and his daughters in California. In between his family visits, he took cruises and trips worldwide.

My grandfather's life story knowingly and unknowingly showed me two crucial things: 1) never give up, even in the face of the world's most abject form of injustice (the Holocaust), and 2) you can always start a new company or a new business, or simply start anew. You have the power to build something out of nothing, no matter what circumstances life hands you. His story was the epitome of the American dream.

> *You have the power to build something out of nothing, no matter what circumstances life hands you.*

Put in these terms, it is no surprise that my mother ultimately married my stepfather, Daniel Levin, one of Chicago's most pioneering real estate developers. My stepfather pioneered the development of affordable housing and mixed-income housing throughout the Chicagoland area for the past fifty years in his role as founder and chairman of The Habitat Company. That said, Dan's most successful real estate venture is the East Bank Club, the largest one-stop-shop fitness facility in not just Chicago but in the country—a company of which he continues to serve as the general managing partner at age eighty-nine. East Bank offers massive athletic facilities; restaurants; a hair salon; dry cleaning services; men's and women's spas; childcare services; tennis courts; takeout food emporiums; yoga studios; quarter-mile tracks, at which Chicago greats like Oprah Winfrey exercise; Olympic-size pools, in which former mayor Rahm Emanuel swims; and even a basketball court where former president Barack Obama plays. Dan is masterful at understanding his customer—whether it's a tenant in a public housing or market-rate development or a member at East Bank. More on that to come.

In my teenage years, I heard my stepfather's stories about his business activities during Sunday night family dinners and during summer internships in college, when he graciously drove me downtown each morning and home each night. I'd watch him take 5:00 p.m. meetings with his East Bank Club management team over a glass of scotch and nibbles. I learned his style of "walk-around management" through direct and indirect observation. He also has shown me time and time again that breaking bread matters (see chapter 5).

Both my grandfather and my stepfather were powerful role models in my life, albeit one allegorical and the other more tactical. Even as a young woman, I knew I could start a business or run a business, because starting businesses and running businesses were just what people did. This is the power of mentorship (see chapter 6).

After two years at Stanford, I'd come to realize I loved three things: Hal, entrepreneurship, and wine. My hobby had turned into a full-blown passion. I wanted to enable people to continue to learn about wine and to do it in a way that was convenient and easy, just like when we gathered at the Wine Circle to get educated about French champagne, Napa Valley cabernets, or New Zealand sauvignon blanc. I saw potential and, before long, the catalyst for a new opportunity—one that would change the course of my career.

To launch my first company, I deployed a series of strategies that can be applied to any business, product, or service:

1. Build a company to last, not to sell.

2. Find an industry you're passionate about; then fix what's broken.

3. If you're a consumer product start-up, defray the inventory carrying cost so you can grow more efficiently.

4. Leverage technology to match people to products.

5. Romance the consumer with a personal touch.

6. Think outside the box for clever marketing plays.

7. Don't be too proud to take an existing idea or concept, personalize it, and use it again.

8. Leverage the halo effect of a compelling and enduring brand.

THE BUSINESS OF WINE

To understand the origins of Bottlenotes, Inc., you first need a little background on the wine industry.

The business of selling of alcohol in the United States is the only category that required *two* amendments to the US Constitution: one that prohibited its sale and one that repealed its prohibition. Selling wine in this country is like selling to fifty different countries: all the state rules are different. There's inherent tension between the Twenty-First Amendment to the US Constitution (which renders states control over the distribution of alcoholic beverages within their borders) and the (dormant) Commerce Clause, which says no state can discriminate against another vis-à-vis interstate commerce in the United States of America. It's a highly regulated industry, to say the least. Keep this in mind, because it will become important in chapter 2.

In 1999, a group of well-to-do venture capitalists and Amazon.com funded something called Wineshopper.com. They were trying to be the Amazon of the wine world. Wineshopper built a front-end website and back-end warehouse. They spent tens of millions of dollars in fewer than nine months to create an infrastructure to legally sell wine through the supply chain governed by the Twenty-First Amendment. Their goal was simple: build it fast, take it public, and become a success story like Drugstore.com.

Wineshopper essentially said, "We're not going to change the US Constitution. We know that in every state, you have to sell from a winery or importer to an in-state distributor, retailer, or restaurant before you sell to a consumer. You can't just sell direct. But as long as we're willing to go through these requisite tiers in the supply chain, we can find middlemen who realize they're not adding value in our direct-to-consumer model. We'll still sell through them—but they'll agree to take a 2 to 3 percent cut instead of 20 to 30 percent, since they are adding such little value. In the end we'll be able to capture the balance of the margin for ourselves as a marketing fee."

They created this creative business model and sent it to the regulators, and the regulators sent back a letter that said, paraphrased, "We approve! Go forth and conquer."

Unfortunately, when the bottom fell out of the dot-com bubble later in 1999, Wineshopper ran out of cash. The company went down in flames.

Enter Katie (Schumacher) Hoertkorn, a brilliant woman and enterprising entrepreneur and executive whose DHL background landed her on the operations team at Wineshopper. Katie asked herself, "What if we revived $70 million of assets from bankruptcy and refined the Wineshopper business model to solely focus on the supply chain management services—not building front-end websites?" Kleiner Perkins agreed with her approach and provided her with the several million dollars of seed capital, enabling her to resurrect Wineshopper's hard assets from bankruptcy. Katie then became the CEO of New Vine Logistics, the phoenix rising out of Wineshopper's ashes.

Now here I am at twenty-six, a burgeoning entrepreneur, and I stumble across the story of New Vine Logistics while writing a paper for my supply chain management course. I don't see a perfect path into entrepreneurship in health and fitness, and I love wine, but I hadn't cracked the code of a new business model.

Writing the New Vine Logistics case while a student at Stanford's GSB, I had a eureka moment: Katie was doing logistics management for wine, but what if the original model for Wineshopper made sense? There was still a front end to be had, and I thought if we could create it swiftly and successfully, we'd launch and get bought quickly, likely by Amazon or an Amazon competitor looking to enter the wine world. I figured I'd grow the company fast and sell it in a couple of years. A quick, clean single or double: #forthewin.

Leadership Hack 1: One should always focus on building a company that is built to last, not built to flip (sell). The focus on building something enduring is what ultimately will help it get sold.

It was 2005. I was fresh out of grad school, ambitious and eager. Inspired by my stepfather and grandfather before me, I jumped headfirst into my first business. *Leadership Hack 2: Find an industry you're passionate about; then fix what's broken.* I'd found a way to marry two of my great passions: entrepreneurship and wine. I thus cofounded a start-up with Kimberly Donaldson that would ultimately go on to become the leading interactive media company in the US wine industry.

We had officially popped the cork on Bottlenotes, Inc.

BOTTLENOTES: THE EARLY YEARS

Long before Blue Apron and Plated popularized the subscription model of food and wine at home, we built out a subscription service based on a wine club concept. Ours also had a clever twist: we had zero inventory carrying costs for the wine on the shelves at New Vine Logistics, as all products on the shelves was legally owned by our winery and importer partners. *Leadership Hack 3: Consumer product start-ups that can defray the inventory carrying costs will always be more resource-efficient to build.* Since we had no inventory carrying costs, the couple of million dollars of seed capital we raised in the first two years all went toward the website, technology development, our patent-pending matching technology, and customer acquisition/marketing activities to get the business off the ground.

Our original Bottlenotes business model was simple: we sent our customers wine tailored to their personal tastes using patent-pending matching technology. That was the Silicon Valley twist, the tech innovation. In an era when the internet can be used to match people to products, why not take a product that was as complex and opaque (literally and figuratively) as wine and make it more accessible to consumers by taking the guesswork out of what they would like?

We scored the different wines by taste profile. Once our customers completed their personal taste profiles on our site, we used their answers to create an algorithm in a massive spreadsheet that matched consumers to wines in our portfolio that best matched their personal tastes via a mathematical match. With every new bottle we sent to our customers, they'd rate it on a five-star scale, letting us know whether or not we hit the mark. We were using **Leadership Hack 4: Use technology to match people with products.** The more wines they rated, the more we were able to home in on their personalized taste profiles.

The fancy technology term for where we were headed was "collaborative filtering." The system was never fully automated, but even manually rerunning the matching, person by person and shipment by shipment, was gratifying and fun. People were getting wine from boutique and estate producers from around the world tailored to their personal tastes.

It worked. We were able to connect each customer with his or her ideal wine. They loved it. We were educating and entertaining consumers in fun, innovative ways. Before long we had wine clubs ranging from novice to advanced: the Explorers Club, Seasonal Tastings, Little Black Dress Club, Jetsetter's Club, Connoisseurs Club, and Limited Addictions. We were doing well by our wine producer partners, too, helping them get access to this next generation of wine enthusiasts.

We had multiple great ideas during those first couple of years. Once we started to provide a personalized recommendation service, a few of our corporate customers said, "If you're doing this for me, can you provide the same service as a holiday gift for thirty of my clients?" So we built out a small but mighty corporate-gifting platform. This story took place almost fifteen years ago now, but even today, private client services are absolutely how many wineries and wine retailers drive material revenues and profit.

If you're an internet-only business or even a hybrid omnichannel retail business, there's this idea that "the personal touch" is gone. But from my experience at Bottlenotes, as well as the companies I've gone on to advise, I've seen that even in the digital age—and perhaps *because* of the digital age—personal touches still matter. Customer relationships still matter. Thanking people for their patronage still matters. You can outsource your scheduling to AI, but at Bottlenotes we reached out personally to corporate customers and said, "You ordered thirty gifts for your clients last year, and here's what you sent. We noticed that you haven't sent any gifts this holiday season. Would you like us to resend to the same thirty people? Same budget? Same delivery addresses? Same gift messages? Here is this year's selection of similarly curated collections."

That's the power of ***Leadership Hack 5: Romance the consumer with a personal touch.*** Take your customers on a human tour of what's possible so they don't feel so overwhelmed by the volume of choice. Like a sommelier or a restaurant server, you are essentially saying, "Here are the options we think you might like." I don't just mean email marketing or customized newsletters—though we did that, too. The most successful e-commerce companies I have observed and purchased from, and with which I continue to have a relationship as a consumer, make me feel, ironically, that the relationship isn't solely transactional. Poshmark's and Slack's customer relationship marketing and app alerts are among the best that I have seen: daily quotes, simple tips, fashion reminders, and comments or quotes that make you chuckle. Ironically, some "big technology" companies like these are the best at ongoing content-relationship marketing.

At Bottlenotes, we made the bet that the next generation of wine consumers wanted access to undiscovered, hidden-gem products tailored to their personal tastes. We quickly found that, while there were certainly some suppliers who were sexist, ageist, closed-minded, and difficult, some were open-minded enough that they were willing to take a chance on working with an emerging platform like Bottlenotes and two young, female entrepreneurs like Alyssa and Kim. We amassed a portfolio of over two hundred wines, and we never owned the product. Every bottle stayed on the shelves of the warehouse— and that model is what enabled us to launch and achieve the very beginnings of scale.

In year two of the company, Limited Addictions was featured in the *Robb Report*. I'll never forget the day a woman from Washington, DC, called and said, "I saw you in *Robb Report*, and I'd like to order twelve bottles a month for my husband."

We couldn't believe it. A woman we'd never met wanted to spend $1,000 a month on wine that we, a fledgling Silicon Valley start-up, had sourced. We were building our brand and expanding in exciting new ways. We were thrilled.

Next up: the Academy Awards.

BUILDING A BRAND TO LAST

In our second year of business, we had the opportunity to sponsor a prolific swag event leading up to the Emmys and Oscars. The PR agency had asked us for a hefty sum if we wanted to attend. We didn't have the money.

Enter *Leadership Hack 6: Think outside the box for smart marketing plays.* You don't need a massive budget to get massive exposure. Don't be too proud to barter.

"We can't deliver thousands of dollars," I said, "but we *can* deliver thousands of dollars of wine to pour at the event, and we can give you gift memberships to our Limited Addictions wine club for your category winners and runners-up."

The agency took the offer. We made beautiful blue Bottlenotes envelopes—a riff on RedEnvelope's collateral back in the day—with a designed, printed message that read: "Welcome to Bottlenotes! Your wine club membership awaits." *Leadership Hack 7: If someone thought of an idea first, don't be too proud to personalize the concept and use it again.*

Weeks later (post-Oscars), I was in the Bottlenotes office in Palo Alto in the front foyer, no shoes on, kicking my heels up at around 6:00 p.m. on a Friday. The rest of my team had gone home for the day, and I was about to leave myself. Then the phone rang.

A very deep, familiar female voice said, "May I speak to Alyssa Rapp, please?"

We would eventually feature Geena Davis in our Bottlenotes newsletter, interviewing her at her home in LA. She was—no surprise for those of us who are fans of her work—a total class act. I have nothing but the greatest admiration for all the pioneering work she's done. Geena was decades ahead of her time in addressing the gender gap, let alone the pay gap, of women on screen and in the media. She used the opportunity of being featured to promote her Geena Davis Institute on Gender; we benefited from the alignment with an A-list Hollywood celebrity who was a member of one of our wine clubs. *Leadership Hack 8: Leverage the halo effect of other people's audiences when scaling a brand.*

By then, the Bottlenotes business model had lots of strong legs. We had conceived, fund-raised, and built a team to pursue a "Netflix for Wine" e-commerce strategy. We had developed a compelling subscription service with different-level wine clubs, from the entry-level Explorers club at $22 per bottle, featuring everyday drinking wines, all the way up to Limited Addictions' $100 wines. We had leveraged our *BottleNews* e-newsletters to organically attract over twenty thousand subscribers, featuring celebrity interviews and other news about wine in the wine world. We also had a corporate-gifting platform and curation through the Bottlenotes Wine Registry, on which we had partnered exclusively with WeddingChannel/The Knot after a soon-to-be-married club member asked us to curate a starter wine cellar for her, sparking the idea.

We'd also created a Winecyclopedia, a "wiki for wine" that had facts and stats. This Winecyclopedia served as the foundation for my first book, *Bottlenotes Guide to Wine: Around the World in 80 Sips* (© Adam's Media 2008). I partnered with the W Hotels and Kobrand Corporation on the book tour—the W hosted and catered, and Kobrand underwrote a flight of six gorgeous international wines for all book launch events. Suddenly we were hosting events for up to two hundred people. I remember thinking, "People like this content, and they like learning about wines from around the world in a walk-around tasting, just like they did in my Stanford Wine Circle days."

It was an exciting and fulfilling time. I had carried on the family tradition and started my own business. My whole life I'd felt the urge to create things—it's why I fell in love with modern dance choreography in high school and kept it going through Yale. I had poured my business and creative minds into a Silicon Valley start-up that was on its way. Bottlenotes wasn't perfect, but it was an innovative firm in the US wine industry that was starting to gain traction. At the time, we thought we were on track to sell the company and get our first single. We were wrong. By 2008, we were getting going as a start-up, adding value to an array of wine producers by leveraging technology to help them target and attract the next generation of US wine consumers.

I had *no idea* that our worst nightmare was about to strike.

CHAPTER 2

PIVOT VERSUS QUIT: WHEN THE GOING GETS TOUGH

Hacks 9–14, Summarized

LEADERSHIP HACK 9

Acknowledge fear, and move through it. Fear gets a bad rap, but it's there for a reason: to protect you from something. Just like standing on a balance beam is scary because your life or limbs are at risk, so, too, is making a business decision like to pivot versus quit, which carries huge risk. Your job is to acknowledge the fear—to take note of its presence—and then push through it. Fear is a normal human response. The trick is in not letting it dominate your psyche.

LEADERSHIP HACK 10

Commit to finishing what you start. You have to commit before you even begin. To quote my dear friend and now world-famous athletic coach Abdul Sillah, "Start strong; finish stronger." Such is true in athletics and in life. If you start anything knowing you probably won't succeed, then you won't; you're setting yourself up for failure. You have show up with full commitment, having faith, true grit, and belief in *yourself.* Does that mean you're going to be 100 percent successful? No. But to paraphrase Lin-Manuel Miranda, "You cannot throw away your shot."

LEADERSHIP HACK 11

All great ideas start with *what if*. Never be afraid to ask *what if*, over and over, until you find a solution. Most of the best entrepreneurial innovation in the United States over the past twenty years has been born out of Silicon Valley, precisely because of the constant willingness to ask and re-ask this simple question. Some people's responses to challenges or obstacles are to stop asking questions. If you want to solve a problem, you have to open yourself up to the possibility that change is inevitable, and reframing the problem will present an otherwise undiscovered solution. My favorite question to ask myself as an entrepreneur and executive—a question I even ask my students—is "If not this, what; and if not now, when?"

LEADERSHIP HACK 12

If you want other people to follow you off the ledge, you'd better be ready to lead by example. And that most often includes voting with your feet *and* your pocketbook. If you want your team to be all in, they have to see that you're all in first. That means leading with your head, heart, and feet—and often also means being willing to put your money where your mouth is. I'm not saying empty out your kids' college funds. But if you're asking your team to tighten their belts a little while, you should be ready and willing to do the same.

LEADERSHIP HACK 13

Make sure your team is fully aligned around the same goal, and set out a specific timeline so that everyone is sprinting. In the case of Bottlenotes, the timetable for a pivot was cash constrained: a real limit, not an artificial one. Nor would I ever have asked the team to work for minimum wage for an indeterminate time frame, which is unrealistic. The pivot worked in part because I gave a finite deadline—ninety days—to us all, and we hit it. We all rowed hard those ninety days, but we always knew exactly where we were headed and kept our eyes on the prize. You have to be crystal clear with your team when you pivot so that everyone is rowing in the same direction with laser focus in a synchronized manner.

LEADERSHIP HACK 14

You have to be present to win. You can't win a race if you're not competing. So before you do anything else—before you commit to finishing what you start, before you acknowledge your fear and move through it—you have to show up. Showing. Up. Matters.

* * *

In 2008, two major headwinds were coming toward us at Bottlenotes. We were about to experience a shift so seismic, we'd be forced to make one of two choices: pivot or quit.

There's purportedly always a calm before the storm. In our case, the "calm" included a robust list of positive metrics. Bottlenotes was getting a fair amount of market traction in terms of our subscription service (wine clubs), the first national Bottlenotes Wine Registry, and corporate gifting; we had leveraged newsletters and celebrity endorsements. Better yet, after ten years of Amazon flirting with the idea of entering the wine business, they were getting serious. They'd originally put $20 million into what was Wineshopper.com and then, allegedly, another $14 million into building their own wine category by working with New Vine Logistics. Now they were getting serious about entering the industry—and sniffing around us and striking a material partnership deal with New Vine.

From my perspective, my original vision was coming to fruition. I had flown up to Seattle to meet with Amazon, where we were building relationships with their wine team; we were meeting with other potential long-term strategic partners too. Everything was lining up as I had originally envisioned. "Bottlenotes really is my single," I thought. "An exit is going to happen at some point soon—then on to the next."

Remember Leadership Hack 1: Don't build a company to flip it? That was one of the biggest lessons I learned from this period of time. If you're focused on the sale, you're making decisions in the name of short-term wins versus building a company that is built to last.

But I didn't know that yet. What I knew by 2008 was that we were suddenly in a very different climate. While we had raised seed capital in 2005 with relative ease, by 2008, the storm hit when the market crashed at the beginning of the Great Recession.

After the market crashed, venture capitalists were skittish about investing in the wine category. When Lehman Brothers is going down, the stock market is tanking, and people are putting everything into cash and holding on for dear life, they're not so inclined to take the money they were going to put into extra cars or second homes or extra vacations or their kids' college funds and give it to you, the super-high-risk entrepreneur.

On the consumer side, people were "trading down" (albeit not out) in terms of daily luxuries like wine. (In the wine industry, the trend to trade down, not out, helped to catapult some extremely savvy, well-timed, strategic players like Duckhorn Wine Company—which expanded the distribution of its second, less expensive label, Decoy, during the Great Recession—to stratospheric success.)

As for Bottlenotes, we were facing what every other start-up was facing: a macroeconomic meltdown.

That was major headwind number one.

Then something even worse and even more unexpected happened.

The regulators got involved.

In chapter 1, I mentioned wine is a highly regulated industry in the United States—and globally, for that matter. In theory I knew this level of regulation could pose a problem to the Bottlenotes business model, but I was too idealistic to fully appreciate the power this gave the entrenched distributors, which had been a protected class in the supply chain since Prohibition in the 1930s.

Then something even worse and even more unexpected happened. The regulators got involved.

Instead of seeing the market as a growing pie, the established distributors were profoundly threatened by the thought of Amazon's entry. What I believed at the time—and the data supports this claim—is that the US wine industry *was* a growing pie. The next-generation consumer would be more likely to visit a winery or order a wine off a restaurant wine list if he or she had tried it at home first. The number one influence then and today on what wine a consumer buys is what they've tried previously and liked. It's why tasting rooms work in Napa: approximately 10 percent of people who visit Napa Valley tasting rooms end up joining wine clubs.

But the distributors didn't see it this way. They were afraid that the pie was fixed, and you were either drinking that bottle of sauvignon blanc at your home on a Tuesday (bought from Amazon) *or* buying it at a restaurant on a Thursday. I subscribe to an alternate viewpoint: a consumer is more inclined to buy a wine that they have tried and liked than one that they have not tried. That said, most terrifyingly to wholesalers, they were afraid that Amazon would ultimately act as a distributor and sell it to restaurants and retailers themselves. (With the Whole Foods acquisition, due to their buyer power and unmatched consumer audience, and legally through Whole Foods' ability through off-premise retail licenses to sell direct to local consumers from each store, they might very well disintermediate traditional wholesalers over time.)

But this was a decade ago, not today. I still remember the day we got wind that an industry advisory was coming our way, calling into question the existence of third-party marketing firms. Their goal was to chase Amazon out of the market—but we at Bottlenotes were collateral damage. While the agency wouldn't be able to regulate us as an unregulated entity, they were creating huge disincentives to work with us. Wineries would be charged major fines and risk losing their licenses if they did business with third-party marketing firms during this strange two-year period, putting their whole livelihoods at risk.

The rules of the game that everyone from Kleiner Perkins— and Alyssa Rapp and Kim Donaldson—had so carefully researched had now changed. All due to the power of the wholesaler lobby and regulators trying to put their heads in the sand about the technology revolution underway.

I had several advisory board members—and family members—say to me, "You gave it the old college try, Alyssa. A noble effort. You didn't lose. They just changed the rules of the game. You thought you were playing checkers, and now you're playing chess. Time to pick a new game."

I was facing a decision I'd never faced before: pivot versus quit. So I pulled out a whole new set of hacks, cranked up the volume, and pushed on—even harder.

9. Acknowledge the fear, and move through it.

10. Commit to finishing what you start.

11. Never be afraid to ask "What if" over and over.

12. If you want people to follow you, lead with your feet *and* your pocketbook.

13. Make sure your team is fully aligned around the same pivot, and set a specific time limit to reach the end goal.

14. You have to be present to win.

STARING DOWN THE FEAR

For me, the decision to pivot versus quit is deeply personal. You have to listen to your inner voice. There's a fine line between knowing when to push through the fear and when to pay deference to it. Fear exists for a reason. It's trying to protect you from something. I learned that on the balance beam.

Fear exists for a reason. It's trying to protect you from something.

I trained as a gymnast from ages seven to seventeen, typically in the gym three hours a day, six days a week, for most of those years.

Being a gymnast was the hardest and most impactful decision of my childhood. When I was on the USGA elite track, I had to deal with dedication, drive, goal orientation, and teamwork. I learned about success, failure, success, and failure, over and over again. Through these experiences, I gained an ability to manage fear, which has been a fundamental building block along my entrepreneurial journey.

The two hacks I learned as a gymnast are applicable to any aspect of life. They're certainly true when you're pivoting, whether you're a big company or a lone entrepreneur. As a gymnast, it's the first and most important thing you have to learn to do: acknowledge your fear and then move through it.

As a sport, gymnastics is all about muscle memory. Your body is doing things that could kill you during any given trick, at any given moment. As a gymnast, repetition is your friend. You can beat fear into submission through repetition. But it never goes away completely.

I still remember what it felt like to stand on the balance beam, about to do a back handspring/layout step-out/back handspring on a piece of wood ten centimeters wide and four feet above the ground, covered in beige leather. I was literally staring fear down my nose every day for ten years. The truth is my stomach churned every single time I stood at the very end of the balance beam, trying to squeeze those three moves into the narrow confines of the width and length. But I acknowledged it. With a deep breath and a one-two-three countdown in my head, I said, "Hi, fear. I acknowledge you. You're right there, and I'm just going to do what I need to do."

It's the same with business. For a pivot or any big business decision to work, you have to have the stomach for it. The fear isn't going to go away: that's part of the package. But you don't have to let it win. *Leadership Hack 9: Acknowledge the fear; then move through it.*

The second lesson is about committing. In gymnastics, commitment is paramount. You're standing with your toes dangling at the end of the balance beam, staring down, doing the same "psych up" that you'd do every time. *Count to three, breathe in, breathe out—then go.* If you stop in the middle, that's when accidents and injuries happen. Your only choice is to visualize, commit—and then go for it.

Leadership Hack 10: You have to commit to finishing what you start before you even begin. There's no other way to do a scary maneuver in gymnastics—and no other way to pivot in business. Whether you have two hundred employees or five, you have to be all in. Sure, circumstances may blow up in your face anyway. But if you don't go in expecting it to work, ready to give it everything you've got, then you'll have no opportunity to win.

A little more than a decade after I'd stopped gymnastics, I was just shy of thirty, an entrepreneur with my first company on its way—and now everything I'd built with Bottlenotes was being threatened.

I thought back to those early days as a gymnast and realized how invaluable those lessons were. What I'd learned about managing fear would be crucial to what we would do next.

PIVOT VERSUS QUIT

I grew up in a Democratic home with the belief that American democracy was good and government could do well by people. My mom was the US ambassador to the Netherlands from 2009 to 2011, having been appointed by President Obama. My stepfather's father was a federal judge. My younger brother met his wife while they were both working in the Obama White House. I myself had been a director of finance in the early part of my career for the indomitable US congresswoman Jan Schakowsky. The people I knew who worked in government were driven, committed, caring, and hardworking people.

When the California regulators at the Alcohol Bureau of Control got a bee in their bonnet about third-party marketing firms, it was my first experience of government gone wrong. This regulatory shift was poised to crush everything we had worked so hard to build. Worse, their policies were anticonsumer, antiwinery, antitechnology. They had forced our hand, leaving us little choice but to raise the white flag or pivot.

We chose to pivot.

Maybe it was all the friends and family from whom we had raised money, people we didn't want to let down. Maybe it was the team who had worked so hard for us for two and a half years. Maybe it was the athlete in me, that thirteen-year-old girl staring down fear, refusing to quit.

Rightly or wrongly—probably both—I said to myself, "We're doing something valuable in the marketplace. We are helping educate and entertain the next generation of wine enthusiasts. Bottlenotes is their trusted source of information, and they're coming to us and getting great wine information they can't access elsewhere. We're also helping wineries and brands get access to this next generation of wine enthusiasts, thus matching supply and demand, which is especially crucial in the context of the unpleasant hourglass shape of the US wine industry's supply chain."

Side note for those of you interested in the wine industry: Today it's even *more* consolidated than it was ten years ago, with two consolidated distributors controlling 90 percent of the ever-growing pie of consumers (defying all sensible antitrust logic, IMHO). It's a practical chokehold.

Once I realized that, there was really only one question: What if we inverted the hourglass—and thus our business model?

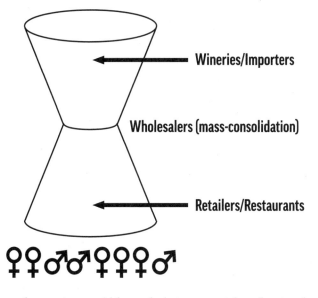

Up to that point, we'd been helping provide value in the supply chain by helping supply meet demand. We were an e-commerce company that made money by providing great wine recommendations to consumers who chose to transact with us, predominantly in a subscription context, online. But what if we shifted our position in the value chain? Instead of consumers paying us, what if we could educate and entertain our audience via the platforms and channels we'd already established—email newsletters, interactive events, social media, mobile applications, and everything else we'd started to build or brainstorm for the last two and a half years—and instead get paid when brands paid us for access to this very qualified audience of self-identified wine enthusiasts, about whom we already had tons of data? In short, to pivot from an e-commerce concept to a new media business model?

Leadership Hack 11: All great ideas start with "what if."
Never be afraid to ask what if, over and over, until you find a
solution.

Despite the macroeconomic meltdown, it was a good time for online media companies. DailyCandy, founded in 2000 by Dany Levy as a daily e-newsletter, had over 2.5 million subscribers when Comcast purchased it for $125 million in 2008. And one of our amazing board members at Bottlenotes, Heather Stephenson, had built IdealBite, an email newsletter business about all things eco and green. She sold it to Disney on the promise of it becoming the leading eco-green brand throughout their empire, digitally and through their physical Disney Worlds. (While her sale was awesome economically, Disney ran IdealBite into the ground two years later, proving that only the rarest of major corporations can throw gasoline on a team's entrepreneurial fire versus snuffing it out.)

At that moment in history, DailyCandy, IdealBite, the *Huffington Post*, and countless additional online media companies were flourishing. This was our best chance of avoiding the *Titanic*.

So in the middle of 2008, I brought in our team. I sat them down in our front office, looked them in the eyes, and embarked on the hardest professional conversation I'd had up to that point. I explained to them that the world as we knew it was changing. And then I gave them my version of a Saint Crispin's Day speech:

"We have two choices, folks. We can quit, or we can sail to a new island. We can hit the wall, or we can pivot and go forward. I'm prepared to go forward—so here's what we're going to do.

"We're not throwing in the towel. But business as we know it will have to cease operations in the next eight weeks. We're going to wind down our e-commerce business quickly so we don't put our partners' licenses at risk. If our clients have a gift membership or someone prepaid, we'll have to send them all the wine at once.

"I have a new vision for Bottlenotes. We're going to continue to educate and entertain consumers and help brands get access to this audience, but we're going to take what were cost centers—our events and our email newsletters—and turn them into profit centers for the business. We're going to turn *BottleNews*, our email newsletter, into a digital email publication (eventually called *The Daily Sip*). We're going to be an interactive media company, educating and entertaining consumers about wine via digital content and live, interactive events. At our *Around the World in 80 Sips* events, we will—true to form—be pouring over eighty different wines from around the world.

> *We're going to take what were cost centers—our events and our email newsletters—and turn them into profit centers for the business.*

"To do this, we need fresh capital and new board members. I'm prepared to put all the money I currently have toward funding this three-month transition. We'll go out and raise money from new investors so we can make a complete transformation. What we need from you are two things: true grit and faith.

"If you can give us both of those things—if you're all in—then you're going to have to tighten your belts. I'm not asking you to give us a lifetime. I'm asking you to give us ninety days to make this pivot and avoid the iceberg. What that means, practically speaking, is that we will need to ramp everyone down to minimum wage for the next three months. Presuming all works out as intended, the company will pay you the delta between minimum wage and what you would have earned, plus interest, when the raise is done and we are on our way. Most of all, you'll have experienced something that great life stories and lessons are made of, particularly in Silicon Valley. But what we need to know is if you're in or you're out, because if you're in, we are rowing hard with barely enough water, provisions, or time.

"And if you can't stomach this transition? No harm, no foul. My Rolodex is open to you. I'll help you find new jobs in this industry—there's no call I won't make, no recommendation letter I won't write, because I appreciate your loyalty to date. I'll do whatever I can. But what we have *no* bandwidth for is wondering whether you're going to jump ship. We'll have barely enough food, fuel, and water to row us all the way to the next island. If you need to go, I completely understand, but we need to know that now. Are you in, or are you out?"

Not a single person walked out of the room.

A week later, one woman decided she didn't have the stomach for it; she'd already been thinking about going into business for herself, so she left Bottlenotes to start her own graphic design agency. Bottlenotes became one of her first clients. But everyone else tightened their belts and rowed like hell.

I dipped into my own funds to make the transition. Some people thought that was a bad idea at the time, but I refused to accept the Silicon Valley mantra of "only spend other people's money." As a Midwesterner, I had a different approach. If you're not willing to bet on yourself, then why should other team members take the risk? ***Leadership Hack 12: If you want other people to follow you off the ledge, you'd better be willing to lead with your feet and your pocketbook.***

As it turned out, the minimum wage pay cut lasted less than ninety days. I can't say I'd ever been prouder than when the funding came in and the company paid team members back their accrued payroll balances, with interest. Our team had bet on themselves—and they'd won.

BE PRESENT TO WIN

The pivot was successful. Bottlenotes transitioned beautifully. We became the leading digital media company in the United States for wine, and later, a pioneer in multiple beverage categories, through digital newsletters and large-scale interactive events. I became an author, publishing my first book, *Bottlenotes Guide to Wine: Around the World in 80 Sips*, and frequently served as an expert on wine/entrepreneurship on national television and in national digital publications, including the *TODAY Show*, the *Rachael Ray Show*, Fox Business Network, and more.

But the success of the transition wasn't about me. It was about our team's decision to stick with the company, to bet on themselves, and see a vision through. I picked the destination, but we all got there together. For a pivot to work, there has to be a shared vision, a high degree of (almost maniacal) focus, and an ability and willingness to persevere. What made it so gratifying was that our team had made the right bet. They had bet on themselves—and they'd won.

It's possible if you believe it's possible, but you have to fully commit. You *all* have to be all in. ***Leadership Hack 13: Make sure everyone you're with is fully aligned around the same goal and you're all rowing in the same direction.*** And give yourself a time limit so that everyone is sprinting. Our team understood it was going to be hard. They understood they'd be out of breath, which tends to be uncomfortable. But they also knew it wasn't going to last forever.

There's one more hack I learned from our decision to pivot, and it's a vital one. Whether you're launching a start-up, changing your strategy, or making any important business decision, you don't have the luxury of resting on your laurels. You have to keep battling, innovating, *out*innovating, and outworking your competition. One of my dear friends, Emily Melton, managing partner and cofounder of

Threshold Ventures, reminded me you have no chance to win a race if you're not standing at the starting block. She coined *Leadership Hack 14: You have to be present to win.*

After a decade of blood, sweat, and tears, I'd cofounded a start-up of which I was proud. We'd pulled together a terrific team, which had in turn pulled off a successful pivot. In 2013, Bottlenotes received the Best Advertising and Marketing Company and the People's Choice Awards at Empact100 at the United Nations, honoring the top one hundred companies with founders under thirty-five. We had arrived at the next rung on the entrepreneurial ladder.

On a more personal level, I was tired. I'd squeezed every ounce of blood from that proverbial stone, and I didn't regret a minute of it. But I'd had my first daughter, Audrey, in 2012, and I would have my second daughter, Henriette, in 2015. I wanted more time not running around like a headless chicken with my feathers on fire. I wanted to lead a business where I wasn't worried about a massive payroll obligation. I wanted something new, something different.

The tide was about to turn.

CHAPTER 3

THE TIDE ALWAYS TURNS: HOW TO TRANSITION WELL

Hacks 15–21, Summarized

LEADERSHIP HACK 15

Your identity doesn't come from titles, degrees, accomplishments, or successes. Your character is defined by *who you are within*. It can be easy to let our value get bound up in the different roles we play: parent, spouse, CEO, etc. But your identity goes much deeper. If you can establish that early on, you'll be able to transition better, because you won't be leaving your entire identity behind when you move from one job (or career, or relationship, or house) to the next.

LEADERSHIP HACK 16

Bet on yourself. I'm extremely fortunate to have been raised in a family that role modeled for me that faith in self and betting on oneself professionally are not the exception but the norm. But even if you didn't get that kind of messaging as a kid, you can learn how to bet on yourself. You are the one person whose effort you can unequivocally count on. Even if nothing else is within your control, if you can commit to putting in honest effort and true grit, you're a wise bet.

LEADERSHIP HACK 17

Be open to the organic next steps professionally. This is true in business and in life. Whether you initiated the transition or it's been forced onto you, *you* don't have to force the next thing. You always have the power to be open and courageous as you take an honest look at what could organically unfold.

LEADERSHIP HACK 18

Take care of your people, and they'll take care of you. It's good practice to *always* take care of your people, but this becomes especially true during a transition. Establish an open dialogue and clear lines of communication, and then check in often to see how people are doing, what they need, and what they're thinking. If you can create a mutually beneficial transition plan, everybody wins.

LEADERSHIP HACK 19

If you want to learn, teach. I may be borrowing this one from Buddha, but it's true. It's one of the reasons I said yes to my Stanford class: I may "lecture" my MBA students, but in teaching them, I learn.

LEADERSHIP HACK 20

Never say never. We all know the saying, "When one door closes, another opens." It's trite, but like it or not, it's true. Try not to slam doors behind you or burn bridges; you never know when you might need them. To quote my mother, "Just because someone cannot help you doesn't mean they can't hurt you."

LEADERSHIP HACK 21

Listen to your heart and your gut when picking a professional path into which you will transition. If you're moving in the wrong direction, chances are either your heart or your gut is going to let you know. Instead of shutting down those inner voices, listen to them. Be open to your heart tugging you in a different direction. If you tune in to your deeper intuition, you will often find the right path.

* * *

As I contemplated how to transition out of Bottlenotes, I started reframing the idea of "conscious uncoupling" (propelled to national vernacular by Gwyneth Paltrow and Chris Martin, although coined by therapist and relationship expert Katherine Woodward Thomas) in a business context. I began to admire the notion of an "uncoupling" from a start-up that had dominated my professional identity for over a decade—and I realized that this very concept was exactly what needed to happen with me and Bottlenotes.

After our daughter Henriette was born in March 2015, I knew I was ready for a change. I was in a very different mood than ten years earlier when I'd cofounded the company. As an entrepreneur, I knew I loved to create. But Hal and I had just created these two small humans, and I wanted to give them 100 percent while also giving my work 100 percent. As a start-up requires 200 percent of yourself just

47

to have a fighting chance to win, I knew the short-term phase of my work life was not congruous with founding another company from scratch.

We've all heard the nightmare stories of bad transitions: exits gone wrong, bridges burned, leaders stepping down after being disgraced by scandal, or founder CEOs being forced out of the very companies they created. Transitions can go well—or poorly—whether dealing with companies or human beings.

As for my post-Bottlenotes years, I wanted to do it right. I found myself looking inside myself for previous life lessons that would help me transition openly, directly, and collaboratively at this new life moment. Here's what I found:

15. Define your true worth and identity, not from external forces but from within.

16. Bet on yourself.

17. Be open to the next steps professionally as they evolve *organically*.

18. Take care of your people, and they'll take care of you.

19. If you want to learn, teach.

20. Never say never.

21. Listen to your heart and your gut when picking a path that makes the most sense for you.

TWO KINDS OF BREAKS

One of the interesting—and challenging—things about transitioning is that it calls into question your identity. If I was no longer

Alyssa Rapp, intrepid entrepreneur and founder of Bottlenotes, Inc., who was I?

In transitioning away from my first company, I realized this wasn't the first time I'd made a big life transition. I found myself looking back to a very specific experience in my life.

When I was seventeen, I went sea kayaking near the Boundary Waters of Minnesota with Outward Bound. A fundamental part of every Outward Bound adventure is the "solo camping" experience: twenty-four hours with no food—just water, a tarp, some string with which to tie it up, and a plethora of pen and paper.

I put that pen and paper to good use. Seventeen-year-old me was channeling Lin-Manuel Miranda's *Hamilton*: "Why do you write like you're running out of time?" It was pouring rain, and I sat under my tarp and wrote and wrote and wrote. I wrote to my mom, to my brother, and most of all, to myself. I'll never forget the things I said in those letters, things I didn't fully understand until I put them down in ink. From an identity standpoint, it was a seminal moment. It was extremely poignant, realizing how much of my identity as a human being had been wrapped up in being a gymnast, a dancer, a student, a sister, and a daughter. At that point, "gymnast" was the most dominant.

What I gleaned from my two weeks sea kayaking, especially the solo camping experience, was that I was who I was *because of who I was from within*. If you stripped away all the hats and titles I wore, all the good grades and positive feedback from gymnastics coaches and teachers—those core values would still be there. ***Leadership Hack 15: Your true worth and identity aren't made up of your accomplishments, titles, degrees, or successes. Character is defined by who you are within.***

What was prescient about that epiphany was that, exactly two months later, I had a horrific, career-ending gymnastics injury doing a Gienger on the uneven parallel bars two weeks into my senior year season. My arm bent ninety degrees one way, turned—I'll spare you the gore. As you might expect, that ended my state-winning prospects. There was even talk that I would never have full use of my right arm again. At the time, the shattered identity of my life as a gymnast was as jarring as my shattered arm. These were heavy realizations on all fronts. I took my Yale college interview three weeks later with a *RoboCop*-style cast/contraption in our living room.

Due to my time alone in the wilderness, I was able to face that transition with more grace and calm than I ever would have been able to otherwise. The injury killed any chances of my doing gymnastics in college—and also came with a huge silver lining. I still remember what I said to my mother as I was being wheeled to the OR for surgery: "Don't ever let me do this sport again."

"Don't worry," she said. "You won't."

After a decade of being stuck in a love-hate relationship with the sport, it was forcibly over. I could channel all of the good stuff I loved about gymnastics into contemporary dance instead. I would take dance with me to Yale, where I danced twenty to thirty hours a week with Yaledancers. Some of the women I met there are my closest friends to this day. In high school and later in college, I doubled down on choreography, which I had always loved but never had enough time to fully pursue. Dance would figure into my adult life, too: from 2007 to 2018, I served on the national board of trustees for Hubbard Street Dance Chicago, the country's preeminent contemporary dance company.

Long before that, when I was a senior in high school, recovering from my injury and expanding my love for dance, I choreographed a piece to Mendelssohn's *Fingal's Cave Overture*, in which water was a metaphor for change. At its heart, the piece was about this turning point in my own life. I was transitioning into the next thing, and dance was a pivotal part of that journey. It also gave me the incredible opportunity to let the people in my community help pick me up again. The break of the arm (and my break with the past) led me into this new phase. The title of the piece was "The Tide Always Turns."

A decade and a half later—during the time of transition from Bottlenotes—I found the silver medallion that my dancers in that piece had given me, with The Tide Always Turns inscribed on it and the date of our first performance of the piece (1996). Fittingly, I was reminded of that transition and what it meant in my life. I would make a decision to approach the next transition with the same openness, a reminder that the tide not only always turns, but transitions will flow more seamlessly if you consciously swim with them.

> *I would make a decision to approach the next transition with the same openness, a reminder that the tide not only always turns, but transitions will flow more seamlessly if you consciously swim with it.*

THE BIRTH OF AJR VENTURES

After exiting Bottlenotes, there was never any question what I was looking for in the next phase of my career. I wanted to do interesting, project-based work with people I enjoyed and admired, working forty to sixty hours a week versus eighty. And I wanted to capitalize on a decade of knowledge and leverage my expertise. I wanted to have maybe one to two people working for/with me (I would ultimately end up with a floating team of four). This is how AJR Ventures was born.

Ironically, AJR (my initials) was the name I originally thought of when I pulled a tax ID for my first start-up. That company would be renamed to Bottlenotes when Kim and I cofounded the company. Ten years later, my thought for AJR was that it would be a little bit of a lot of things. I invested in a handful of trademarks for different start-up ideas I had. (For a sneak peek into ZenHen, Peak31, BottleBar, and more, check out www.alyssarapp.com to unlock special online content.) I made a teeny angel investment in one artificial intelligence company. But principally, I provided advisory services to private-equity-backed companies or family offices looking to turbocharge their growth via e-commerce, digital media, new product innovation, or other 360-degree go-to-market strategies.

It never occurred to me *not* to bet on myself. I thought, "I built some great relationships and have a decade of great learnings from the school of hard knocks; now I'm going to take the leap and assume some firms are going to want to leverage these learnings and insights." That belief in myself has been pivotal at all the key moments in my life: falling in love with my husband, starting Bottlenotes, and ultimately transitioning out of Bottlenotes. The truth is betting on myself in my own case doesn't feel like a choice; it just seems embedded into who I am, how my mother raised me.

Leadership Hack 16: Bet on yourself. If you know you can count on your effort, if nothing else, it's a wise bet.

AJR Ventures evolved in a totally organic and satisfying way. There were some small projects I did for friends who were colleagues whom I wanted to help; I kept them short, just in case a big fish came along. Sure enough, one did: a private-equity firm in Chicago brought me in to develop a US go-to-market strategy, including an e-commerce strategy, for a portfolio company specializing in men's luxury apparel. That was a six-month project for four of us that could have taken six of us a year. That was an extremely satisfying, one-off advisory gig. ***Leadership Hack 17: Be open to the organic next steps professionally. If you approach that "what if" with openness and flexibility, you'll be better equipped to adapt and evolve.***

What I learned from that experience was how much I enjoyed juggling multiple projects and diving into new industries. In athletics you talk about going hard and then taking a day to recover. There was nothing "day off" about this. I certainly wasn't slowing down. Within weeks of launching AJR, I had three big projects.

Full disclosure: I've never been good at taking time off. I'm still not great about it. As George Lucas's *Star Wars* series reminds us through almost all lead characters, one's strength is also at risk of becoming one's greatest vulnerability. For me, I don't see limits time-wise. Obviously there comes a point where there are diminishing returns, when you are literally and figuratively spreading yourself too thin—versus just focusing on one thing into which you pour everything. With AJR Ventures, I was genuinely enjoying the fact that I didn't have a massive payroll to meet. I had more ownership of my schedule, just like I'd wanted. I was spending quality time with my daughters and my husband. I was still giving 100 percent to my work but avoiding overextending into that 1,000 percent place that start-ups often require.

If you have people working for you, you always need leadership skills to be successful. But at the end of the day, AJR didn't require a big leadership vision. That's one of the things what was so great about it: instead of solving problems in my own company, someone else was presenting me with *their* problems to solve. I got to think

> Instead of solving problems in my own company, someone else was presenting me with their problems to solve.

through them and then bring in other experts so we could problem-solve together. The people with whom I had the great fortune to collaborate ranged from former Bulldogs on the Bay summer interns like Jinying Yang and Anthony Overstreet and longtime friends and advisors like Tracy Wan, to new friends like Ann Peltz and Sonia Hunt. These collaborations were what I enjoyed most in the AJR Ventures advisory years.

With AJR Ventures I "de-risked" my life a little bit. At the same time, I had to bring home the bacon and drum up my own projects, so it wasn't exactly risk-free. During those three years, I was reminded of how much I enjoyed building teams from scratch populated by deeply talented people. Anthony Overstreet was the one person who traveled with me from Bottlenotes to AJR Ventures, and he remains one of the best hires I've ever made.

Anthony originally started as my marketing and operations summer intern at Bottlenotes in 2012. He quickly scaled the ranks, becoming operations manager in 2013, senior operations manager in 2014, and director of operations in 2015. Around the time I was ready to leave Bottlenotes, I knew Anthony and I were both thinking about what would come next.

I didn't want a big fleet of people, but I was willing to take on one mouth to feed, and Anthony was extraordinary. He was my number two at AJR Ventures. He helped do a ton of the research and preparation for multiple projects, which I never could have done solo. We collaborated well, and he was literally my right-hand man.

The entire time Anthony was at AJR, we both knew it wasn't his end game. We kept an open dialogue on a rolling basis of the projects we were working on together and, for him, what was next. I was pushing him to go to business school, and he said he wasn't ready or didn't want to go. When he finally got clarity on what he wanted, he realized that what he wanted next was to transition to big tech.

Out came the Rolodex. I said, "Let's get you your dream job." Now he's a product specialist at Facebook, where he's been for over two years.

Anthony's transitions were textbook utopic, first from Bottlenotes into AJR Ventures and then ultimately out of AJR Ventures to Facebook. They were collaborative and symbiotic. For me the biggest reminder with Anthony was the power of open, honest communication, including updates on how something is going. As a result of that authentic relationship, we were both instrumental in each other's lives. Anthony helped me, and I helped him.

Leadership Hack 18: Take care of your people, and your people will take care of you.

GIVING BACK

In 2015, everyone in Silicon Valley who'd had a massive exit with dollars dripping from the sky wanted to teach and advise. But when I started teaching at Stanford, I didn't do it from an optics standpoint. I did it because I was a brand-new mom again and wanted to try to make it at least a year, maybe a year and a half, nursing. Stanford was only a mile from our house, so I would drop our daughter off at her nursery school on campus and then drive four hundred yards to my office—an ideal situation for the whole family.

Teaching was my way of leveraging more than a decade of experience and expertise and giving back to the larger community. I knew I had something to offer, and it was gratifying to be able to do so. I'd been playing with the idea of teaching for a while—in 2012 one of my Yale Bulldogs on the Bay summer interns had asked me to put together a syllabus to teach a course at Yale on the economics of the global wine industry. While I was inspired enough to create a syllabus and meet with the master (now head of college) of one of Yale's residential colleges, I was running a company, newly married, and even more newly pregnant. I had to face the facts: teaching a course across the country that would require a six-hour plane ride plus a two-and-a-half-hour drive would be a little aggressive (as Hal reminded me).

Instead, I asked the beloved admissions director at Stanford GSB at that time, Derrick Bolton, if there was someone at Stanford University with whom I could be in touch about the possibility of teaching a strategy class through the lens of wine. He graciously put me in touch with the GSB's then–associate dean, Madhav Rajan, who even more graciously said he was happy to test run the course that year on a half-quarter basis—and he thought it would be even better if I'd be willing to teach it with a tenured faculty member. Professor Michael Hannan (now a professor emeritus) was a great copilot. He taught me the rules of the road at Stanford, a gilded academic institution. He cautioned me against the temptation to cram in as much as possible for fear of running out of content. Instead, he encouraged me to be "comfortable giving the class enough room to develop robust conversations." Five years later, I'm still working on implementing this great life lesson from Professor Hannan.

In April 2014, I joined the ranks as a lecturer in management at Stanford University's Graduate School of Business. I also advised multiple independent studies—even when it meant extra time working with students simply out of the goodness of my heart. I had a strong desire to blow oxygen on the embers of their entrepreneurial dreams, as so many faculty members had done for me.

For five years, I have taught the course to a packed audience of over fifty students. Dynamics of the Global Wine Industry examines the world of wine with a fresh and contemporary perspective, providing insight into the branding, marketing, and distribution dynamics that shape what and why consumers buy and consume. In addition to a weekly lecture and/or discussion via the Socratic method on a particular case, I host a guest speaker, including wine industry icons such as Peter Mondavi Jr. (the youngest son of Peter Mondavi Sr.) of Charles Krug, Napa's oldest winery, and Christine Wente of Wente Vineyards; mavens like Duckhorn Wine Company CMO Carol Reber; and entrepreneurs like Terry Wheatley of Vintage Wine Estates. Each student receives his or her own custom One for All wine glass by Gabriel-Glas, an elegant and durable glass that maximizes the bouquet and enhances the aroma of every style of wine. As you'd imagine, it's been a very popular course.

For the first couple of years after moving back to the Midwest with my family, I continued to teach at Stanford, taking an early flight into San Francisco every Thursday morning and a red-eye back to Chicago or to another East Coast destination for Surgical Solutions every Thursday night for nine consecutive weeks from January to March. The schedule can be punishing, particularly by weeks eight and nine. The upshot is I got more work done in the "quiet" solitude of four hours and thirty-one minutes on United Airlines than I ever could have with my iPhone in hand and team members right outside my office. Without question I couldn't and wouldn't do it fifty-two weeks a year as the toll is too great on me physically and on my family. But for one quarter—nine consecutive weeks—it was worth the sacrifice.

Why? Because teaching a case once a week, whether I wrote it or not, forces me to sharpen my intellectual tool kit, to think at the hundred-thousand-foot versus the hundred-foot (tactical) level. The gift of teaching in a top academic environment like Stanford's GSB is the quick wit, depth of thought, and ambitious nature of the students. The global strategies we deliberated had a spillover effect for how I approached even the health care industry. And the performer in me loves to be back "on the stage" for three hours, nine weeks in a row, as a lecturer in management at a top business school.

I teach because of the satisfaction that comes from a student coming up to me after class saying, "This was the best class I took at the GSB." Or "I wish there were more [women] lecturers like you." Or writing in a farewell class-blog post, "I had no idea that the best strategy class I took at Stanford would have been through the prism of wine. What we discussed is applicable to so many other industries." After a decade of toiling in Silicon Valley as a female entrepreneur in luxury consumer products (wine) and technology, I wanted to believe that the school of hard-knocks learning would have legs—and inspire lives—beyond those touched by my first company. My last semester at Yale, I took a class on screenwriting that forever impacted the way I "consumed" film, and I hoped to inspire a class each year to view wine differently, to let the learnings from my course influence their future travel decisions, purchasing decisions, and even career decisions.

If I could inspire one or more students each year to follow his or her dreams and take the career road less traveled, all the better. Knowing someone else's life trajectory might have been impacted makes all the 4:00 a.m. wake-ups and 11:00 p.m. red-eyes worth it.

Leadership Hack 19: If you want to learn, teach.

THE NEXT STEP

When Hal's father passed away—the ultimate catalyst for us leaving the half of our lives in the Bay Area—AJR Ventures was flourishing. I'd put a lot into it and was working with great people on great projects. I was always surprised when people said to me, "So you've started two companies, Alyssa?" The way I saw it, I'd started one company (Bottlenotes), and now I was doing advisory work. Nevertheless, it was in a way becoming another company, my next "baby." When the time came to move to Chicago, I had to do what was right for my flesh-and-blood family. I'm grateful for the choice we made to uproot our family and move everyone back to Chicago full time. It felt right then and today.

It wasn't just about my family either. It was also about what felt right for me professionally. I had taken enough time to advise and look "from the outside in" to other companies and other executive teams and help them strategize about how to build products or brands or divisions of companies or companies themselves. But I was ready to be back in the captain's seat. The AJR Ventures years taught me that I loved working on great projects with great people—and that I love to teach—but I was ready to be a CEO again.

What do I love about being a CEO? First and foremost, I love to lead teams. I loved it in my gymnastics era, I loved it in my dancing years, and I love it as a professional. I also love to interact with a board of directors—to "manage up and manage down" in an organization. I love that I have the responsibility to impact multiple functional domains: finance, operations, marketing, sales, business development, technology development, human resources, corporate development/strategic partnerships, and so forth. I love to put a stake in the ground on a strategy and be responsible for its execution and implementation. I love to try to inspire people to all row in the same direction toward the same big, hairy, audacious goal. The truth is, I like a big challenge. Always have. I gravitate toward the burden of the responsibility. I like a job that involves engagement with multiple stakeholders, like our private-equity partners and my team. I like being the one at the helm of the ship.

Not too long ago, someone asked me, "How would you feel about serving as the general manager of a billion-dollar division of a multibillion-dollar company versus serving as a CEO?" I said, "I'm super flattered you thought of me, and that's an interesting question to which I do not have an immediate answer." But as the saying goes in Silicon Valley, sometimes entrepreneurs are considered fundamentally "unemployable"—we are not happy if we are not iterating on the next idea or company that we will start or run ourselves. I love the variety of the CEO job itself, the buck ultimately stopping with me. Heretofore, I have found the job function of CEO to be most satisfying way to meet those professional objectives. That said, I have also learned enough by now to know ***Leadership Hack 20: Never say never.***

One thing I learned as a dancer and choreographer was that transitions are just as important to a piece's fluidity as the beginning or the end. That transition out of Bottlenotes into AJR Ventures was neither perfect nor easy. But it was exactly what I needed when I needed it. I knew intuitively when it was right to start pulling back on company one and seamlessly transition into company two. For me that phase of transition was about doing what I knew in my gut and heart was right. ***Leadership Hack 21: Listen to your heart and your gut; then pick a path that makes sense for you.***

Now, years later, I was ready to hack a new industry, to incisively understand a problem and solve it. As we transitioned back to Chicago full time, I knew career change would be coming with it. I still never expected what I'd be doing next.

CHAPTER 4

SURGICAL SOLUTIONS: HACKING THE HEALTH CARE INDUSTRY

Hacks 22–32, Summarized

LEADERSHIP HACK 22

Being a good leader doesn't mean talking all the time. Sometimes the very best thing you can do as a leader is to *not* talk. Shut your mouth, keep your eyes and ears open, and let the people around you share their experience and domain expertise. Watch and learn.

LEADERSHIP HACK 23

There's no substitute for looking people in the whites of their eyes. You can't always get out in the field and meet your team. But whenever you can, do it. There's something powerful about being physically present with other people, looking them in the eye, and building an authentic human connection.

LEADERSHIP HACK 24

Assess your people. A lot of good leadership is about assessment. You can't move forward until you do an honest and fair assessment of your people. Who's aligned with the company's goals and mission statement? Who isn't? Be honest with yourself so that you can be honest with your team. Which of your people are costing you valuable time, resources, or energy?

LEADERSHIP HACK 25

Hire slowly; fire quickly. There's a reason this is common wisdom at the nation's top business schools. When you bring people on board, take all the time you need to make sure they're a good fit. And when it just isn't working, call it what it is. Be fair, be reasonable, follow the law, and do what's right—but also don't be afraid to swap out people. When I've stalled on firing someone and I finally do, I always wish I'd made the call months prior.

LEADERSHIP HACK 26

Deep dive into your industry. Until you have a working knowledge of your industry, you won't be able to move forward with acumen and resolve. Experience comes with time, so while you're logging hours, do everything you can to learn about your industry and any ripple effects moving through it. Read books. Read articles. Interview people. Think of yourself like a sponge, where your responsibility is to soak up everything you can.

LEADERSHIP HACK 27

Establish thought leadership. For you and your company, this might be a white paper or a series of think pieces you publish on your blog. Maybe it's a partnership with an influencer on social media. Whatever your industry, there are ways to establish thought leadership, so be on the lookout for good ones. And when friends or colleagues make suggestions, listen. They might have a great idea that hadn't occurred to you.

LEADERSHIP HACK 28

Find ways to build in job variability and mobility for your team. No one wants to be static. Variability and mobility will look different across industries, but opportunities for movement are always a good thing. Find ways to offer these to your team members in ways that are meaningful.

LEADERSHIP HACK 29

You can't wear every hat—and why would you want to? Outsource. If you spread yourself too thin, you won't do anything well. Stop trying to do everything yourself and outsource the tasks that are a drain on you as a resource. This frees up more time and energy to do the work at which you're best.

LEADERSHIP HACK 30

Stabilize, save, and sell. For me at Surgical, that meant recruiting top talent, extracting costs, re-architecting our sales pipeline, and finding partners. For you it may look different. Just remember to assess what isn't stable first so you can work to correct it.

LEADERSHIP HACK 31

Find ways to incentivize productivity. People perform better when given proper incentives. Set up an incentive structure that is intuitive, smart, and aligned with the desired results.

LEADERSHIP HACK 32

Design the system for the behavior you're seeking. Your incentive structure should be bespoke, something you've created with specific behavioral benchmarks in mind. Clarify those benchmarks for yourself first and then for your people. Then design a system that "connects the dots" between the work and the results.

* * *

When I started my tenure as CEO of Surgical Solutions, I'd never worked in health care a day in my life.

On day five of the job, I arrived at my first hospital site visit with my chief clinical advisor and account manager. I showed up in high heels with a roller bag, fresh off a red-eye—and had to jump into scrubs and get behind the scenes with our team in less than an hour.

I snapped a selfie in the OR and sent it to Dr. Amanda Munoz, my childhood best friend who is a Harvard Med School-trained, Stanford ENT resident/fellow and current ENT surgeon.

"Hell hath frozen over," she wrote back. "You could barely get through the fetal pig dissection in AP biology without screaming. How on earth are you running a health care company?"

Amanda wasn't wrong. I was a babe in the woods in the health care industry—and I had to lean hard into *Leadership Hack 22: Keep your mouth shut and eyes open. Watch and learn.*

But let's rewind a bit. To understand how Surgical Solutions itself is innovative in the US health care industry, providing a service that helps hospitals operate more profitably by pushing an array of fixed costs to variable costs—a health care industry hack, if you will—you first have to understand how the story began and how I came to be a part of it.

From my early conversations with Steven Taslitz, chairman of Sterling Partners, I knew I would have a unique opportunity to work with an entrepreneurially minded private-equity firm as a CEO of one of their portfolio companies. While our conversations over several months included an array of possibilities, from coffee to women's health and more, I was eager to run something $20–$50 million in revenue, and Sterling was in need of a CEO for Surgical Solutions. Whatever reticence I had about health care was overcome by Steven's and Sterling's long tenure in building, growing, and managing portfolio companies; in the depth of experience and easy communication dynamic with my board chair, Ancelmo Lopes; and in the deep domain expertise and awesome mentorship provided by other tremendous directors, Jay Istvan and Cherilyn Murer.

That said, there was a lot I *didn't* know. Over the next two years, I would leverage an array of leadership hacks that not only transformed the way I led the company: they transformed the company itself.

22. Keep your mouth shut and eyes open. Watch and learn.

23. Whenever possible, meet people face to face, and look them in the whites of their eyes.

24. Assess your people while being both fair and honest.

25. Hire slowly; fire quickly.

26. Do a deep dive to understand your industry and industry trends.

27. Establish thought leadership in smart, innovative ways.

28. Find ways to build in job variability and mobility for your team.

29. You're never going to be the best at everything, so be prepared to outsource.

30. Stabilize, save, and sell.

31. Incentivize productivity.

32. Design the system for the behavior you're seeking.

IS THERE A *THERE* THERE?

In the year before I arrived at Surgical, there had been a fundamental change in strategy at Sterling Partners. To the surprise of many stakeholders within the firm and outside, the portfolio company had decided to reorganize. While Sterling would continue as a private-equity firm to manage their current funds and holdings (of which Surgical Solutions is one), they would not seek to raise a fifth fund, which was a pretty dramatic change in strategy. The decision inspired an exodus of many of Sterling's longtime executives who were the next-generation leaders at the firm. Some left to start new funds, with Sterling's direct and indirect support. Some stayed.

While Sterling's decision to evolve into a hybrid family office/private-equity firm was not the expected path forward for some of the longtime former lieutenants, it was a highly attractive partnership structure and organizational design for someone as entrepreneurial as I. The shift in traditional structure not only didn't scare me, but I actually found it appealing. The deals Sterling would continue to be part of on the family office side were very interesting to me—and a good fit for my consumer roots. (They have incubated a series of consumer internet companies internally under the umbrella of Eighty-Seven.) With Steven's blessing, the original Sterling health care team had spun off to launch their own health care fund; as a result, Surgical was orphaned for a while. Steven ended up stepping into this investment as one of the lead board members. That's when he recruited me.

"Alyssa," he said, "we're both new to this. In the first sixty days, I want you to answer for me one simple question: Is there a *there* there?"

As I said in the introduction, I did plenty of preparation before I started at Surgical Solutions: I read a whole stack of books on change management and the unique challenges of stepping in as a turnaround CEO. I embarked upon social conversations with other people at the company and solicited as much unfiltered feedback as I could before showing up on day one. But at the end of all the prep work, there's still a day one.

When I took the helm at Surgical, they had been lacking a full-time CEO for more than twelve months. This wasn't your usual leadership changing of the guard. And when the lead investor of the firm that owns you—not to mention one of the directors of the company—asks, "Is there a *there* there?" you can't help but wonder, "How can I quickly figure that out?"

To answer this simple yet complex question, I took a multi-pronged approach.

First, I needed to see as many of our existing customers as I could, as quickly as possible. ***Leadership Hack 23: There's no substitute for showing up.*** I had my existing team members take me on field visits to assess our people on the ground as well as our customer relationships. I wanted to look, listen, see, and feel everything I could. It's just like you do with wine: sometimes you just have to experience it to truly understand it.

In those early meetings, I asked direct questions of our customers: "How indispensable are we? Anyone here you just can't live without? If there were one other thing we could do for you that we're not doing, what would it be?" I was trying to understand to the best of my knowledge the strength of the customer relationships we had—and presumably the team would be putting me in front of the strongest accounts up front. On the other side of that equation, it was important that I see how our account managers handled those visits too.

I was always willing to get in scrubs to meet the people in the field who were doing the work from day to day. I met with our implementation technicians—I call them "Surgical SEALs"—and our account managers over cups of coffee or quick bites to eat in hospital cafeterias during their breaks at the hospitals where they worked. My goal was simply to get to know people, listen to their wants and needs, and strive to quickly build trust.

During one visit, I met one of our account supervisors in New York. She took time out of her day to give me the tour, and she was awesome. I couldn't help but notice the running shoes she was wearing because I happened to have the same pair. I complimented her sneakers, and when she talked about needing a new pair, I said, "You're on your feet all day—this job must be wearing you out!"

Once I got home, I sent her a new pair of sneakers, on me. I added a note thanking her for the extremely informative tour. I have found that personal touches and immediately acting on observations can have a big impact: your team knows you are watching closely. They know that you care. Since then, this account supervisor has been promoted and continues to be a rising star in our company.

Second, I needed to quickly analyze, from a team perspective, the people with whom I was compatible and would be able to work, and the people who didn't meet that criteria. ***Leadership Hack 24: Assess your people.*** In a short span of time, I needed to ascertain where the strengths were in the organization and where and what the greatest weaknesses and gaps were. In other words, I was basically professionally "speed dating" dozens of people internally as quickly as I could.

There's a lesson frequently taught at the top business schools that I'm going to borrow for **Leadership Hack 25: Hire slowly; fire quickly (insofar as quickly usually means yesterday).** At Surgical, there were a couple of changes that seemed obvious right out of the gate, and I made those within the first sixty days on the corporate team. There were some that seemed somewhat obvious, but I knew I needed to take time to make those decisions because they'd send seismic quakes through the entire company.

Even though I'd run a consumer internet company in California, this was an entirely new industry in a different state. I had a vast Rolodex—but I didn't have a massive Rolodex of health care executives. I had to recruit a director of finance, one whom we hoped to be able to quickly promote to CFO. Thankfully, a young, rising star on Sterling Partners' finance team, Logan Derck, had perfect finance chops (CPA, CFA, MSA, etc.) and was interested in an operating role at a portfolio company. He in fact did quickly rise to become our CFO, and he's been one of my right-hand partners in the company ever since.

I also knew from the beginning that I needed to bring in more women. We had a head of sales at the time, but we didn't have someone running customer

> I also knew from the beginning that I needed to bring in more women.

experience who was focusing on same-store growth. I hired a woman who had been a health care executive for literally thirty years, most notably in orthopedic sales in the operating room. I sent her around the country to focus on opportunities for same-store growth, places where we could add business units and business lines to our existing portfolio.

I brought on another thirty-year health care veteran who's a treasure trove of knowledge to spearhead business development and special projects as our VP of business development. I brought in my longtime advisor, Tracy Wan, former president and CEO of Sharper Image, to help us get our arms around the company's financial reporting activities and multisite operations at Surgical. Thanks to Tracy's coaching, we put in place systems, processes, and reporting mechanisms that would set us up for transparency in operations and ideally long-term success.

Early on, Logan, Tracy, and I strived to understand which of our "stores" were performing best, which were performing worst, which could be turned around, and which could not. Were our account managers incentivized on their own same-store profitability metrics? What could we be doing at the corporate level to stabilize and save operationally? Traditional operations (and people operations) at private-equity-backed companies are often brutal, given the demands for cost-efficient growth. Surgical Solutions is no exception. I remain in tremendous gratitude for the opportunity to leverage Logan's financial acumen and private-equity background alongside Tracy's depth of operational experience to help drive the ball forward in this crucial phase of Surgical's evolution, setting us up for long-term success.

Third, I needed to gather information. This was the most substantive part of those intense first sixty days. ***Leadership Hack 26: Do a deep dive to understand the industry and industry trends.*** I went to conferences and listened to the experts. I inhaled *Becker's Healthcare Review* (and eventually published my own piece with them). I read everything I could about the new partnership between Amazon, Berkshire Hathaway, and J. P. Morgan: three of the largest privately held companies in the country coming together to create their own health care plans. I was a sponge. And the best way to jump the learning curve was to surround myself with experts, like our chief clinical advisor and ultimately an advisory board of exemplary clinical leaders in the field, all the health care veterans I previously mentioned, in order to absorb their domain expertise.

I had set out to answer Steven's question with a three-pronged approach: go out into the field and see as many customers as I could, assess our people and bring in those who could help me drive change the fastest, and deep dive the industry and the industry trends. You have to pop the hood of the car if you want to figure out how the carburetor works and how the pipes fit together. Only then can you answer the question of what to optimize.

At the first official board meeting, I was able to say, "Here are the things we've done, here are the things we will do, and here are the people I've brought on to do the job." After the wild ride of the first sixty days, I felt confident that there *was* a *there* there. But there was also a tremendous amount of work to be done, and ready or not, it was time for everyone to roll up their sleeves.

First up: Surgical needed some fresh, smart, efficient PR. So I brushed the dust off *Leadership Hack 27: Establish thought leadership.* For us, this would be achieved via a white paper.

SURGICAL SOLUTIONS: A "HACK" FOR HOSPITALS SEEKING TO OPERATE MORE EFFICIENTLY AND PROFITABLY

Surgical had never produced a white paper before. When the suggestion came to me from my then–head of sales, it immediately stuck. I asked my students at Stanford's Graduate School of Business to send an email to the health care club to see if any MBAs would be interested in a paid research position to write a white paper. A couple of months later, I received an email from a newly minted Stanford MD/MBA, Akhilesh Pathipati, who was then a resident in Boston.

He wanted a part-time research opportunity to gain exposure and make some money on the side during his residency.

Akhilesh worked on the white paper for six months in partnership with our chief clinical advisor, Tony Dawson, and me, focusing on two of our customers, Erlanger Health System and Baystate Health. He highlighted how these health care teams benefited from implementing contract service solutions, which we profiled as case studies.

I've talked about my experience "hacking" a new industry, but I haven't actually talked about how Surgical's unique solution is itself a health care industry hack.

First, let me give you a primer on the current landscape. American health care is undergoing a transformation. Changing demographics, technological development, and new policy measures have all affected the ways in which we deliver and pay for care. Perhaps nowhere are those changes more evident than in the practice of surgery. Operating rooms have long been major sources of revenue for health care providers. Yet as the economics of health care shift, health systems have experienced shrinking margins and are continually expected to "get paid less to do more," to quote my childhood friend Matthew Primack, CEO of Advocate Christ Hospital, Chicago's largest contiguous hospital location.[2]

Today's hospital leaders and managers are faced with the challenge of how to leverage new opportunities, mitigate risk, and ensure the delivery of cost-effective care. One solution is to use third-party service providers. A growing number of hospitals have established outside contracts for functions like clinical staffing and supply chain management. Although outsourcing is not a revolutionary business

---

2   Meeting with Alyssa Rapp and Matthew Primack, April 8, 2019, Advocate Christ Hospital.

strategy, its application to perioperative services represents a strategic and adaptive framework for hospitals to improve both patient care and their bottom lines.

In the white paper, we identified four key trends affecting hospital performance:

Trend 1: An aging population will spur increased demand for health care services.

An older population inevitably has greater health needs. The number of Americans with diabetes, dementia, and other chronic diseases will more than double by 2050. This growing disease burden has come with a corresponding increase in the need for surgery. Over the last two decades, the number of surgeries performed in the United States has shot up by 17 percent, and the majority of these are performed on patients over the age of sixty-five.[3] Surgical specialties are expected to see some of the largest increases in demand.

Trend 2: Surgical care is increasingly outpatient and minimally invasive.

Higher surgical volume has been accompanied by changing techniques. One of the biggest drivers of this transition has been the development of endoscopes for minimally invasive surgery (MIS). Scopes allow surgeons to gain internal views of the body with cameras, precluding the needs for large incisions and direct views. Procedures that once required lengthy hospitals stays can now be done on an outpatient basis. The transition to MIS has important implications: from a patient perspective, MIS has led to lower complication rates, shorter hospital stays, and reduced blood loss. There

---

3   Alyssa Rapp, "Outsourcing Is an Essential Component of Operating Room Efficiency," Becker's Hospital Review, accessed August 19, 2019, https://www.beckershospitalreview.com/facilities-management/outsourcing-is-an-essential-component-of-operating-room-efficiency.html.

is little question that increased utilization of MIS procedures can improve patient outcomes.

Trend 3: Health systems are under financial pressure due to policy changes, an evolving payer mix, and rising operating expenses.

Hospital operating margins are nearing all-time lows. An analysis by the Congressional Budget Office found that a majority of US hospitals will have negative margins by 2025 if they remain at their current levels of productivity.[4] Hospitals face rising operating costs, with two costly expenses: technology and labor. Labor is the single largest expense for most hospitals on account of administrative burdens and the increasingly complex business of medicine, which bloats an already overtaxed system, preventing hospitals from improving patient care or expanding clinical capacity.

Trend 4: Health systems face physician and nurse staffing shortages.

Despite increased spending on labor, hospitals are struggling to maintain appropriate levels of clinical staff, in large part due to limited supply. The American Association of Medical Colleges projects a shortage of 120,000 physicians by 2030, and the American Association of Colleges of Nursing estimates over one million nursing job openings by 2024.[5] Staffing shortages are complicated by an epidemic of burnout among caregivers, which leads more employees to quit, creating a vicious cycle.

Into this beleaguered environment comes Surgical Solutions.

---

4   Tamara Hayford, Lyle Nelson, and Alexia Diorio, "Projecting Hospitals' Profit Margins under Several Illustrative Scenarios: Working Paper 2016-04," Congressional Budget Office, accessed August 20, 2019, https://www.cbo.gov/publication/51919.

5   "Nursing Shortage," American Association of Colleges of Nursing, accessed August 20, 2019, https://www.aacnnursing.org/Portals/42/News/Factsheets/Nursing-Shortage-Factsheet.pdf.

The solution we provide a hospital is a shortcut, a way to "variablize" often crushing fixed expenses. Operating rooms are an enormous source of cost and revenue for any hospital. On average, ORs account for 30 to 50 percent of a hospital's expenses and 60 to 70 percent of their revenues. With ballooning surgical volume and rapid advances in operative technology, there is little doubt the OR will continue to command the lion's share of hospital balance sheets and play an outsized role in patient outcomes.

As a result, ORs are particularly sensitive to the trends described above. Thus, OR leaders and managers must find ways to schedule more cases with an ever-changing surgical tool kit amid shrinking budgets and workforce shortages. Efficiency is crucial in this environment. An increasing number of health systems are turning to third-party service providers like Surgical Solutions who can streamline processes and maximize throughput (e.g., serving patients more quickly end to end, setting up and breaking down operating rooms for each case, providing all of the behind-the-scenes decontamination of equipment and instrumentation that will touch the patient, and more).

Contracting OR services saves money by converting fixed costs into variable costs. Operating rooms are expensive. They require investment in core infrastructure such as OR tables, lights, and booms, as well as clinical tools such as anesthesia machines and surgical instruments. There has been a proliferation of new techniques in the last decade, including the development of mini- and microlaparoscopy, single-incision cholecystectomy, robotic surgery, and transluminal endoscopy (in which there is no external incision). These advances are a boon for patients. But for a hospital trying to keep up with the latest developments in surgery, it means writing off older technology, making expensive new purchases, and retraining staff on how to work with different tools. In an environment of shrinking operating margins, this type of spending is often unsustainable.

Surgical Solutions addresses the problem by sharing risk and expanding hospital balance sheets. From a business model standpoint, we provide a bundled service offering with four key components:

(1) Human capital

Our CRCST-trained technicians are painstakingly trained at our offices using AORN (Association of Operating Room Nurses) curriculum; our own corporate trainer, an esteemed surgical technician; and mock OR training with a dummy. After learning in a classroom setting where they can ask questions in a nonintimidating environment, they're then getting that training reinforced through clinical observation and experience.

When we send in our Surgical SEALs to set up a new account, they're the best technicians in the field. They also love what they do. Our people are incentivized; we understand that we don't make money as a company unless we manage our bundled service offering effectively.

(2) Capital equipment/repairs management

Due to advancements in technology, the need to continually upgrade capital equipment is real. These items are often not cheap, nor are the repairs associated with them. When Surgical Solutions purchases or leases equipment to utilize in our customers' accounts, we bundle those fees into our cost per case. In a hospital, things are inevitably going to break, but our repair incidents are significantly lower than average due to expert training and careful handling of equipment by our technicians.

(3) Disposable instrumentation

In laparoscopy cases, we often, although not always, further bundle disposable instrumentation into our cost per case.

(4) Data and dashboards

Surgical Solutions is striving to not only leverage technology to understand our own costs per case on a real-time basis but to be able to share that baseline data with our customers to help them drive operational efficiencies as well.

In summary, hospitals can say to us, "We are going to take all the challenges and costs of hiring and firing and training and staffing and overtime—and hand them to you, Surgical Solutions!" This fact makes Surgical Solutions a health care industry "hack." We're outsourcing these activities so that we can stick to what we do best, which is hiring the best clinicians and caring for our patients. And make no mistake: there's an extremely high turnover rate among technicians. When employed by a hospital versus Surgical Solutions, the job often requires being stuck in a dark, windowless room decontaminating scopes. It's a crucially important job, but it's not everyone's idea of a good time.

At Surgical, however, a technician has job variability. All technicians will participate in preoperative room setup, intra-op support, and postoperative room breakdown, including the decontamination work in the sterile processing division. We've built some variation into the ecosystem so that our technicians aren't just doing the same thing every day—some days you are working in the OR and other days in the sterile processing department. And there's job mobility too—you could start as a technician and end up a lead technician, account supervisor, or account manager. There's upward mobility that typically wouldn't be there in a hospital environment. ***Leader-***

ship Hack 28: Find ways to build in job variability and mobility for your team. If they wake up wanting to go to work every day, everyone wins.

By partnering with Surgical, physicians and nurses are able to perform at the top of their licenses, increasing OR efficiency and provider satisfaction. In other words, while Surgical Solutions provides a cash flow hack for hospitals, we also offer a job satisfaction hack for hospitals, insofar as time that surgeons and nurses used to spend on workflow and logistics can now be spent on patient care. Time that providers spend on workflow and logistics is a drag on OR productivity. This shift helps to improve morale and decrease burnout among clinicians—and of course paves the way for caregivers to provide superior patient care.

From a "hacking" standpoint, at Surgical we further allow the hospital to hack its own processes by risk sharing with us. Given the macrotrends we're seeing in health care, I believe this trend is something that hospitals should—and *will*—be doing more and more.

Every time a Surgical SEAL walks into the OR with white-glove service and attitude, it allows health care professionals to operate at the top of their games, so they don't have to stop a procedure because a video tower goes out when there's a patient on the table. We're there to troubleshoot that for them. If there's a piece of instrumentation that breaks midprocedure or is missing, the Surgical Solutions technician will leave the room to run and get a new one so that a doctor or a nurse doesn't have to do so.

Leadership Hack 29: No matter what industry you're in, none of us are ever going to be the best at everything. Ideally, in addition to cost savings, that's why you outsource. If you're a hospital, you should be the best clinicians and patient-care providers that you can be. So if you're already outsourcing your food service operations or laundry operations, why not also outsource this critical piece of the puzzle, the foundation of which can make you more efficient, productive, and cost effective?

NOW HERE'S THE BAD NEWS

The white paper was a smart move, especially once we started circulating it to hospitals and ambulatory surgery centers to generate leads. We were providing a service that was timely in the ecosystem of health care, and the white paper served as an instant source of credibility, providing an eloquent overview of our value proposition. As I told Steven and the Surgical Solutions board, "The good news is that Surgical has the opportunity to catch the crest of the wave. Our macromarket timing couldn't be better."

Then I broke the *bad* news.

When Sterling had bought the company four years prior, there were no competitors. The largest competitor was insourcing, meaning the hospitals were doing the work themselves. By the time I took the helm at Surgical, three or four of the largest original equipment manufacturers (OEMs) were testing out their own service offerings. Kind of like when you take your car in for an oil change, your dealer tries to sell you additional services. It's a higher margin for the car dealer, but high value in terms of trust and convenience for you, the car owner. Continuing to go to your dealer for service appointments keeps you sticky and loyal, more likely to buy your next car from them.

So at my first official board meeting after the sixty-day analysis, when I told the board that there was a *there* there, I also updated them about the competitive landscape. I said we needed to find some strategic partners, stat. And perhaps most importantly, I needed to extract several million dollars out of our operating expenses. My theme for year one became *Leadership Hack 30: stabilize, save, and sell.*

To do this, I had to extract costs. There were legacy relationships that had not been examined because they were founder driven and people didn't want to upset the apple cart. But since the competitive landscape was changing, I saw an opportunity. Over the first year, I was very proud that we were able to extract millions of dollars of expenses out of the existing operations while completing all of the human capital transitions and business model transformations previously discussed.

Remember how at Bottlenotes I told my team I needed them all to row hard in the same direction? At Surgical, even that wasn't enough. I had to plug the holes and swap out some of the sailors. I called on my executive team to help me turn the ship around.

We had to get people galvanized and engaged to understand the company vision and buy into it. It was important to cultivate an awareness of their ownership, responsibility, and achievement of goals. To that end, we set up an incentive structure that would require extra-hard work—hence the incentive bonus.

Leadership Hack 31: Incentivize productivity. I learned that lesson from Edward Lazear, one of the most famous economists in the country, who chaired President George W. Bush's Council of Economic Advisers. Prior to that, he was one of my favorite professors at Stanford Business School. Lazear was one of the inventors of tournament theory, an economic theory that makes a strong case for tying incentives to productivity.

> **Sidebar for the econ geeks:** Tournament theory is the notion that you will put in an extraordinary effort when the prize is perceived to be extremely high. It's why people are willing to risk their physical and mental health–to basically kill them-

selves–to be in the NFL. Or why Bernie Madoff committed his egregious crimes. When the prize is great enough, some people will do whatever it takes to win.

Incentives are powerful motivators. If you want people to sell more hospital accounts, overpay them for closes. Want only the most profitable accounts? Pay out longer-trail commissions if/when accounts hit minimum profitability thresholds, or have commissions rise alongside profitability. ***Leadership Hack 32: Design the system for the behavior that you're seeking.***

Net-net, year one at Surgical Solutions taught me how to hack the learning curve in a new industry, how to hack a leadership turnaround, and how a mission-critical outsourced service provider can serve as an instrumental hack for its customers. The strategy seemed clear. Now it became an execution game.

Enter: how to manage and inspire your team to help you summit the next operational peak.

CHAPTER 5

BREAKING BREAD MATTERS AND HOW TO MANAGE A BOARD (OR OTHER CRITICAL STAKEHOLDERS)

Hacks 33–43, Summarized

LEADERSHIP HACK 33

Breaking bread matters. When you're sharing a meal, you're connecting on a human level. Hosting people at your home for dinner can be a way to fast-track relationships built on trust and mutual understanding. Even if it's in a restaurant, eating together creates a special kind of bond, one that transcends the boardroom or meeting room.

LEADERSHIP HACK 34

Seek out opportunities for team bonding events. For us, it was cooking a meal together. For you, it might be taking your team to play laser tag.

The idea is to get people out of the boardroom or office and into a new environment, one where they can flex different team-building muscles. It's meant to be fun, but of course every interaction with your team is also an opportunity to observe and learn.

LEADERSHIP HACK 35

Make people feel valued as human beings. Get to know their tribes. If you treat people like tools to be leveraged, you're selling them—and your team—short. But if you get to know them in a real way and are genuinely interested in their lives, it fosters connection and community. Ask about people's families, and acknowledge the big events in their lives. How was Bob's daughter's graduation? Is Jen's brother still in the hospital? How is Tom's wife's new job going? By checking in, people know you care.

LEADERSHIP HACK 36

Sometimes it's the in-between moments that matter. We spend so much time and energy focusing on the big moments in our lives and careers—promotion, weddings, children's births—that we often forget the power of the in between. *That's* where relationships are built and nurtured. As the saying goes, "Life is what happens while you're busy making other plans."

LEADERSHIP HACK 37

Give people homework to inspire them think more deeply about the challenges at hand. No one wants to go to a long, monotonous meeting where their time isn't being well utilized. Find ways to get your people to sit up and pay attention. Don't think of homework as a list of busywork or trivial minutiae. Instead, leverage homework as a way to engage key stakeholders ... especially board members.

LEADERSHIP HACK 38

Send out four strategic questions before every board meeting or another meeting with critical stakeholders. It doesn't have to be four—could be three, could be six—but choose a digestible number, and then stick to it. Naming four specific questions beforehand gives meeting participants something to chew on and will also help you orient and streamline the conversation so it's productive for all parties. By sending homework prior to a major meeting, the meeting itself can be spent in meaningful discussion.

LEADERSHIP HACK 39

Give people time to review the material you're sending, because you want them to read it all. I aim for a full week of lead time. While this goal is not always achievable, I truly strive to give them no fewer than three days. You don't want people to be skimming important content the day of. You want them to give it a focused, deep read in advance of sitting down with you.

LEADERSHIP HACK 40

Communication is idiosyncratic to each individual. Think of your relationships with your people like a nice suit: they have to be bespoke if you want everything to fit. Don't make the mistake of thinking one size fits all. Take the time to learn about people's preferred communication styles, and then tailor your communication dynamics accordingly.

LEADERSHIP HACK 41

Transparency instills confidence. That's true even when what you're sharing isn't positive—in fact sometimes *more* so. If you keep the lines of communication open and are able to frankly state, "Here's a potential problem coming down the pike," that is infinitely better than picking up the phone after the fact to say, "Bad news. We didn't get this under control, and now it's too late." Your major stakeholders are your allies. They need to know when an opposing army is charging down the battlefield.

LEADERSHIP HACK 42

It's always better to overcommunicate than undercommunicate. You definitely want to respect the communication preferences of the different stakeholders. That said, it's always better to err on the side of communicating more rather than less, especially with sensitive subjects. Don't worry about pestering someone. It's better to pester than to let things fester.

LEADERSHIP HACK 43

Be direct. The truth will always come out, I learned early and often from my mother. Be honest about the good, the bad, and the ugly. If people are going to hear the truth anyway, wouldn't you rather be the one to tell it to them?

* * *

My second week at Surgical Solutions, I invited all twenty members of the corporate team into our home for dinner. I wanted to give people the opportunity to meet my husband, meet our children, and see who I was beyond the veneer of an office setting.

As such, I didn't want the event to be catered by a restaurant, as that seemed too impersonal and unceremonious. Nor did I have the bandwidth to run a company and cook for twenty on a weeknight (if ever). Instead, I brought in Chef Miles, a talented friend who was between restaurant gigs and had started moonlighting as a private chef. I knew I liked his style, and I knew dinner guests would enjoy watching him cook. While Chef Miles worked his magic in the kitchen, I sat guests at the counter for cocktail hour. It was fun and conversational, a part of the evening entertainment—and I didn't have to manage the stress of preparing dinner while entertaining at our home.

I *didn't* hire a bartender. The team knew about my wine background, and it was important to me that I selected and served the wines myself. Whenever a guest walked into the house, Hal or I served them their first glass so we could have a quick conversation. Then I walked around the house and poured, serving some great wine and telling some wine-related stories.

The purpose of the dinner was to get to know people in an informal, relaxed setting, with terrific wines and delicious food—the implication being, "If you're coming to my home for a dinner party, we're not colleagues: you're coming as our guests." They met Hal and our girls, and in so doing, they got to know *me* beyond the CEO chair. I'm not some bitch in heels or snob from Silicon Valley. I'm a mom and a wife—and I'm feeding you dinner.

Leadership Hack 33: Breaking bread matters. That's one of many lessons for managing a new team that I've leveraged over the last several years, including the following:

33. Breaking bread matters.

34. Team bonding events like cooking together actually help coalesce teams.

35. Make people feel valued as human beings, not just tools you're leveraging. And don't just stop with them. Get to know their tribes.

36. Sometimes it's the in-between moments that matter. Appreciate them. Leverage them.

37. Give people homework to keep them engaged and make them think.

38. Send out four strategic questions before every major stakeholder meeting.

39. Give people time to review the material you're sending, because you want them to read it all.

40. Communication is idiosyncratic to each individual. Each relationship should be bespoke.

41. It's always better to overcommunicate than undercommunicate.

42. Information sharing and transparency instill confidence, even when what you are sharing is not always positive.

43. Be direct with your board members about the good, the bad, and the ugly.

LEVERAGING THE IN-BETWEEN MOMENTS

Having the team over to break bread wasn't a one-off. Several months after our first dinner, we did another executive team bonding session at our home. This time I didn't bring in Chef Miles. I handled the wine, the setup, and the breakdown—but the team designed and cooked the menu. They assigned different tasks and responsibilities to each person and then prepped and cooked a four-course meal.

At the first dinner, I didn't do seating arrangements. But this time, our daughters created handwritten seating cards. The environment was warm and festive, and as a bonus, I had a chance to see how my people worked together as a team: one person cut carrots, another boiled water; one was bossy, another collaborative; one was more focused on substance than style, another more focused on style than substance; and so on.

Leadership Hack 34: Team bonding events like cooking together actually help coalesce teams. Cliché as it may seem, working collaboratively on a non–work-related project highlights people's strengths and weaknesses, which often strengthens the connective tissue between team members back in the work environment. The result: greater self-awareness, greater interdependency, and more facile communication.

Leadership Hack 35: Make people feel valued as human beings, not just tools you're leveraging. And don't just stop with them. Get to know their spouses, their children, their family members, their tribes. Now that we've established a good rhythm, I try to host a dinner or at least a happy hour with my team every four to six months.

Sometimes you'll get an unexpected opportunity to break bread with your people out in the field, perhaps even serendipitously. A couple of months ago, we had a huge meeting in New England, and five of my executive team members flew out for it. We were all at the Boston Logan Airport two or three hours before our departure time— and then a storm front blew in, delaying our flights back to Chicago. So we five sat at Legal Sea Foods in the airport and had a couple of bottles of wine and just relaxed. We talked about our spouses and kids and what they were up to. We talked about our next planned vacations. Sure, work crept in. But over bowls of clam chowder, we were able to connect in a way that felt easy and conversational.

Breaking bread together puts everyone at ease. Food in general has a way of breaking down boundaries and connecting people. Conversations that may feel dicey around a board table feel less dicey over a glass of wine. ***Leadership Hack 36: Sometimes it's the in-between moments that matter. Appreciate them. Leverage them.***

THE FOUR QUESTIONS

Having been raised in a culturally Jewish environment, I cannot help but think of Passover when someone brings up the "four questions." (At Passover, the answers to the four questions are responses to "How is this night different from all other nights?")

Breaking bread doesn't just matter in terms of team members getting to know each other; it can be a crucial way to congeal a board of directors. A dinner beforehand paves the way for the most conversational dialogue possible in a board meeting. It may even inspire friendships to evolve outside the more formal board dynamics. Having a board dinner the night before a board meeting is a great way to break the ice. We can't always do it because of challenging schedules, but when we can, it's optimal. We catch up personally and check in with one another—and potentially even preview some of the heavier dialogue in one-on-one conversations prior to the next day's meeting. At a board dinner, I get a better sense of where people stand on certain issues. I've found that trust can build in those in-between moments in very authentic ways.

In my experience, managing a group of major stakeholders like a corporate board is both about managing the organism of the board *and* the individual relationships with each stakeholder. Every group's dynamics is based on the personalities of the people. That can actually be a boon—as long as you can bring those personalities together. Look people in the eye, and ask them genuine questions about their lives.

Of course, you can't just drink wine and break bread forever. At some point, you have to turn your attention to the actual meeting.

I'll just say it: meetings are boring unless you're forced to think. And in my experience, the only way I can inspire people to think is to give them homework. My biggest takeaway from—and contribution to—the corporate boards I've been on and led is **Leadership Hack 37: Give people homework to keep them engaged and inspire them think deeply.** Which segues nicely into **Leadership Hack 38: Send out key strategic questions before every meeting.**

It doesn't have to be four questions; that's not a magic number. It could be six. It could be three. But it shouldn't be more than seven or eight because people will get overwhelmed. For me, the four questions are a way to organize the four to six hours. Prior to a board meeting, I send out the discussion questions alongside the one-hundred-plus-page board book. Then we spend our time going through the questions one by one, usually for about an hour each. The way I see it, if I'm paying you to be here and you're really smart and you have a lot of experience, I don't need to sit here and perform a dog and pony show for you. You are incentivized and compensated to synthesize information, provide recommendations, and help mitigate risk. If I can provide you with three to four key areas of focus before each meeting and you can read the preparatory material with these questions in mind, we can then come together and have a productive conversation abound the four key decision areas.

For example, the questions I send out before a board meeting might be, "Should we be pursuing *x* as a distribution channel? Should we be pursuing a 'buy versus build' technology strategy? How should we be reworking the compensation of our sales team?"

In every board meeting, particularly corporate board meetings, there will be perfunctory details. Approval of the board minutes, stock option grants, hiring/firing updates, leases to vote on, etc.—whatever the specifics may be, these are things you need to get through from a business point of view. But these board business items should only take fifteen to twenty minutes from each meeting. (If the list is routinely very long, boards can even consider a consent agenda that requires only one vote for all items within it.) Sending out four bigger strategic questions beforehand is a way to craft the *substantive* part of why you have people together in that room. The expectation is that members have read all the material and synthesized it. Then they show up, think, and have points of view on several meaty topics that could impact the entity's ultimate endgame. That's powerful.

These questions help us use our time efficiently and effectively. I always want to leverage the time of the board members—not to be talked *at* but *listened to*. If they didn't want to be a valued contributor, why would they be spending their time on this board? Why else are you paying them to be there if you don't want to leverage their unique talents and insights?

To that end, I try to get the materials out to everyone a week in advance. I can't always swing it, but even three days is better than one. *Leadership Hack 39: Give people time to review the material you're sending if you want them to read it all.* If so, you're setting yourself up for a board meeting where you're maximizing key stakeholders' contributions to the meeting.

ESTABLISH CLEAR LINES OF COMMUNICATION

Managing key stakeholder relationships one-on-one is absolutely crucial. But there's no written code for how they should look—every relationship has to be customized and personalized.

Surgical Solutions has board meetings every two months, but I inevitably connect with each board member individually in between, some once a month, others once a week. I have a standing call every Monday with my board chair. It's our weekly visit, our time to catch up and connect. He also joins us on a lot of team calls at his discretion, but we've established a cadence of weekly one-on-one calls, with texts and quick phone updates in between.

My contact with Steven Taslitz, the chairman of Sterling Partners and the majority shareholder in the company, is more sporadic. He travels extensively and is pulled in a million different directions. My general rule of thumb for Steven is that when he calls or emails or texts, I respond immediately. If I've got his attention for a period of time, I try to leverage it.

Also keep in mind that sometimes it's good to get people out of a professional setting. In the same way that having team members over to my home for dinner helps strengthen relationships, I look for other ways to connect with major stakeholders outside the meeting room. I recently said yes to an invite from an advisor to attend an Eagles concert with two board members and two team members. It sure beat an office or boardroom, and we got a lot done. Plus, we had a blast! Next up: I said yes to join an alternate director as her guest at a fashion show.

As you can see, these relationships are not one size fits all. Maybe you're having weekly lunches with a major stakeholder. Or maybe you're meeting with a board member's daughter who's graduating from college and needs a female CEO role model, and you're staying connected to your board member that way. ***Leadership Hack 40: Communication is idiosyncratic to each individual.*** Each relationship should be bespoke. Get to know each stakeholder's communication style. Some people like to get short bursts of weekly insights. Some people don't. The cadence will evolve organically with each individual, as long as you get to know your board members as human beings.

At Bottlenotes, we wrote really extensive monthly investor updates that ultimately whittled down to quarterly, but they were eight to nine pages with section headers. Whether providing investors with financial updates, operational updates, marketing updates, sales updates, human capital updates, return on investment updates—we provided the facts and management discussion and analysis because we wanted to not only inform but educate them. We could have just updated the financials and provided little else to meet our disclosure requirements. We chose to provide color commentary because we thought it helped strengthen our relationships with investors.

Leadership Hack 41: It's always better to overcommunicate than undercommunicate. Reach out by text or email. Schedule intermittent breakfasts if you sense there's interest. And remember to be consistent. One thing about investor relations I've learned is that when you have a key investor, you never want them to be wondering, "What's going on over there?" Remember that these are very, very busy people who have given you their treasure (financial or time) to shepherd and grow. You have a responsibility to keep them informed on a real-time basis.

Never be afraid to pick up the phone and send a quick update on a positive development—or a *not*-positive development. Everyone likes to see and hear about the wins. But if you establish clear lines of communication early on, when there *is* a hard conversation to be had, you've already laid the foundation to have it. (That said, good news usually travels the fastest.) *Leadership Hack 42: Transparency instills confidence.* If there's something difficult brewing, pick up the phone and engage their counsel along the way. That's not only for self-preservation—it's so they can be part of the solution. You never want to get to a place where key stakeholders say, "What? I thought everything was going perfectly, and then you pulled the rug out on me."

Your instinct may be to sweep these things under the carpet. But that's exactly when a spark becomes a brushfire. Rather than pussyfoot around a tricky issue, it's better to be honest. In my experience, people meet that honesty with more gratitude and respect, precisely because you're not obfuscating the truth. ***Leadership Hack 43: Be direct with your board members about the good, the bad, and the ugly.*** As my mother continually taught me: "The truth always comes out. You might as well tell it from the start."

CHAPTER 6

BE ONE, GET ONE: ON MENTORSHIP

Hacks 44–54, Summarized

LEADERSHIP HACK 44

When seeking a mentor, take initiative and do your homework. There are plenty of potential mentors, but you have to do the work to find them. Make use of the resources available to you, whether that means creating an account on a site like findamentor.com or going to industry conferences or trade shows. Put yourself out there, and don't feel shy about approaching your heroes or the people that you admire. The worst they can say is no.

LEADERSHIP HACK 45

Clarify what you're looking for in a mentorship ... and ask your mentors what *they* want out of the relationship. First, get clear with yourself about what you want out of this relationship. Someone who will take a hands-on role in your career? General encouragement? Then convey that information articulately and honestly to your potential mentor so she or he can see if you're a match.

Your mentor may want nothing in return, or they may solicit your unique insight or skill set. You won't know unless you ask. This will help you establish early on the playbook for the mentorship: who's getting what from whom.

LEADERSHIP HACK 46

Find someone who is personally invested in your success. You want a mentor who cares about you on both a professional and personal level, a mentor who can wholeheartedly cheer you on.

LEADERSHIP HACK 47

Be conscious of time … and continually thank your mentor for his or her impact on your life. Your mentor's time is valuable, and he or she is sharing it with you. Be respectful and mindful of that gift. When you say you're going to show up somewhere, show up. On time. And a little gratitude goes a long way. I make a point to thank my mentors often for everything they've done for me, whether that's through a handwritten thank-you note or small tokens of appreciation (gifts) unique to them. These people have affected your life, often in powerful ways. Thank them for it.

LEADERSHIP HACK 48

Showing up matters. Lay out ground rules and expectations for your communications, establish parameters, and set clear boundaries with your mentees. Have a candid conversation about these topics so that the mentorship is built on crystal-clear expectations.

LEADERSHIP HACK 49

Be an active listener. The backbone of good mentoring is good listening. Listen well, listen long, and listen hard.

LEADERSHIP HACK 50

Do what you say you're going to do. When you make a commitment to your mentee, whether it's to show up at lunch, review their proposal, or write them a letter of recommendation, *always* keep your word.

LEADERSHIP HACK 51

Find someone to make you his or her protégé. This fits neatly into a chapter on mentorship—and it's all the more crucial if you're a woman. Your mentor will act as a kind of coach, someone who will inspire, guide, and support you by providing introductions and opportunities throughout your life. One connection can change your career trajectory forever.

LEADERSHIP HACK 52

Support flexible work environments. This can be a challenge, especially at a smaller organization. In my experience, if you give employees flexibility around pregnancies and raising children, they show up to work even more committed, loyal, and effective.

LEADERSHIP HACK 53

Do your best to eradicate sexism in America. We're *all* responsible for creating the kind of environments in which we want to live and work. The good news is, we've arrived at the moment when the women entering the workplace today are proud to call themselves feminists. It's incumbent upon men and women to foster this sense of equality, whether that means going to marches, writing articles, or calling people out for being sexist or misogynist. Women in leadership positions are in unique positions to support other women.

LEADERSHIP HACK 54

Be the change you wish to see in the world. Gandhi said it best. If you want the world to be a better place, do everything in your power to make it so.

* * *

We live in a golden age of mentorship. According to a survey by the American Society for Training and Development, a remarkable 75 percent of executives say mentoring has been critical to their career development.[6] Bill Gates had Warren Buffet. Sheryl Sandberg had Larry Summers. Even Oprah Winfrey, a woman who has mentored countless individuals herself, had Maya Angelou. "She was there for me always," says Winfrey, "guiding me through some of the most important years of my life."[7]

I wholeheartedly believe in the power of mentorship. I have never shied away from asking for help and advice at important decision-making junctures in my professional life—and I'm happy to be able to give help and advice to others who ask for it. Simply put, no matter where you are in your career, you don't need to go it alone.

> *I wholeheartedly believe in the power of mentorship.*

As a mentee, I have benefited from the deep experience of people who have made a personal investment in my career. I'm lucky to count Marissa Mayer, the iconic Google engineer and former

---

6   Alyssa Rapp, "Be One, Get One: The Importance of Mentorship," Forbes, accessed August 19, 2019, https://www.forbes.com/sites/yec/2018/10/02/be-one-get-one-the-importance-of-mentorship/#1d27e0b17434.

7   Carolyn M. Brown, "Oprah to Pay Special Tribute to Maya Angelou," Black Enterprise, accessed August 20, 2019, https://www.blackenterprise.com/oprah-to-pay-special-tribute-to-maya-angelou/.

Yahoo! CEO, as one of my dear friends and mentors. When I faced the decision about leading a firm that someone else had founded in an industry brand new to me, Marissa's guidance was instrumental. She was endlessly generous with her time, helping me to analyze the opportunity and a few others, particularly in terms of compensation relative to shareholder value and returns, and with overall empathy and encouragement. For her never-ending willingness to answer the call for advice—no matter how much she has on her plate—I am continually grateful.

As a mentor, I, too, attempt to provide a spirit of willingness and generosity. I hope to help accelerate other peoples' learnings and career growth, simply by investing time and insight. To do so is incredibly gratifying. When I take the time to mentor someone, my company or organization often benefits from this relationship.

You get as much out of mentorship as you put in. That is why I joined the national board of the Spark Program, whose mission is to provide life-changing mentorships to middle schoolers (www.sparkprogram.org).

Of course, not everyone has a mentor—even when they want one. In a recent study, Kabbage, Inc., a global financial services, technology, and data platform, surveyed more than two hundred small-business owners in the United States. What they found was striking: 92 percent of the people they surveyed agreed that mentors have a direct impact on the growth and survival of a start-up or company. Yet only 22 percent of small-business owners had mentors when they started their business—and 89 percent of those who didn't wished they did.[8]

---

8   Alyssa Rapp, "Be One, Get One: The Importance of Mentorship," Forbes, accessed August 19, 2019, https://www.forbes.com/sites/yec/2018/10/02/be-one-get-one-the-importance-of-mentorship/#1d27e0b17434.

Fortunately, there are a number of ways to ensure you don't end up among those statistics. If you are seeking mentorship, there are people in your field or industry looking to mentor promising and ambitious individuals. You just have to find the right match.

Through my own experiences as both a mentee and mentor, I've learned a number of highly effective hacks:

44. If you're serious about finding a mentor, take initiative—and do your homework.

45. Ask your mentors what they want out of the relationship.

46. Find someone who is personally invested in your success.

47. Thank your mentor for the ways they have impacted your life ... and be respectful of his or her time.

48. Showing up matters.

49. Be an active listener.

50. Do what you say you're going to do.

51. Find someone to make you his or her protégé.

52. Support flexible work environments.

53. Do your best to eradicate sexism in America's business environment.

54. "Be the change you wish to see in the world" (Gandhi).

BUILDING A MENTOR RELATIONSHIP OVER TIME

If the thought of finding a mentor feels daunting, don't let it. Because of how interconnected we are today, it's never been easier to seek out a mentor and establish a fruitful relationship. *Leadership Hack 44:*

If you're serious about finding a mentor, take initiative—and do your homework.

Depending on whether you're an extrovert or introvert, you can always start on the World Wide Web. There are dozens of online matchmaking services designed to pair mentors with mentees. Websites such as findamentor.com will allow you to connect with people in your area of expertise. The internet has the added benefit of bridging geographical distance. Maybe your dream mentor doesn't live in your city, but you could set up a regular video check-in call.

Networking events are another great way to seek out a simpatico relationship. Depending on your industry, you might find potential mentors at trade shows, conferences, or speaking events. Social media has provided another terrific avenue for connecting. Are you following any leaders, innovators, or trailblazers on Twitter or LinkedIn? DM them. Maybe they won't respond, but maybe they will. The onus is on you to reach out. To paraphrase a line from *Twelfth Night*, some are born with mentors, some achieve mentors, and some have mentors thrust upon them. You should always assume that you will *not* have a mentor thrust upon you. You have to do the work, find the right person, and ask the right questions.

Once you've identified someone you think might be a good match, be straightforward about what you want and need. ***Leadership Hack 45: Clarify what you're looking for in a mentorship.*** What you have in mind may be totally different than what they have in mind. Maybe you're picturing a mentorship where you meet every Friday and have specific agenda items to address, whereas they're imagining an informal arrangement where you grab lunch every six months. Do you want advice? Encouragement? Regular check-ins? Brainstorming sessions? Hands-on guidance? Help balancing work and life commitments?

Of course, for the mentorship to thrive, you also want to give the mentor what *they* need. Ask your mentor what they want out of the relationship. Some people may want to give back without asking for anything in return, a way to pay it forward after being mentored in the past. Others may in fact have something you could help them with in their own lives. If you're both open to a two-way mentorship, great. There's no right or wrong way to craft a mentorship. You both get to decide what works for you.

Once you settle on a mentorship strategy that works, allow room to grow. In the same way you will evolve as a person, so, too, will your relationship. What you need *right now* will be different than what you need six months from now, which will be different than what you need in two years. Be up front about how your needs may change over the arc of your relationship, both in ways you expect and ways you can't predict. This will help your mentor help you—and together you can adjust your plan as you continue to adapt and evolve.

It's invaluable to have a mentor whose journey is complementary to yours. **Leadership Hack 46: Find someone who is personally invested in your success.** Mentors should also be willing to be open and honest about their experiences so you can truly learn from them.

Christie Hefner is one of my most cherished mentors for several reasons. She's brilliant, strategic, civically and politically engaged, and extremely knowledgeable about media and business—not to mention a pioneer of women's rights. When we meet every few months, I share my goals, ask for her input and advice, and benefit from her introductions and feedback. I feel fortunate to count her as one of my mentors, not just because she is a great leader, but also because she is always emotionally available and present when we meet.

One thing I've found to be profoundly important in my own mentor relationships is *Leadership Hack 47 (Part 1): Be conscious of time.* I mean this in two respects. First, take the wheel when it comes to scheduling a meeting. It's general practice that the mentee is responsible for reaching out to the mentor with a scheduling request, so put reminders in your calendar, and stay on top of it. Because there will inevitably be times when your mentor needs to reschedule, remember to be flexible.

Which brings us to the second respect: respect your mentor's time. They are no doubt juggling a rigorous and demanding schedule—if they weren't, you probably wouldn't have sought them out. And yet they are giving their valuable time to you. Don't abuse the privilege. Arrive at meetings on time. Respond promptly to all correspondence. If there are action items you've agreed to do between meetings, do them.

Mentor relationships aren't instantaneous. They grow over time. As you learn about each other's lives, both professionally and personally, be genuinely curious and respectful. Try not to focus on what this person can get you, and instead think about building an authentic connection. Don't be afraid to be vulnerable, but also remember that vulnerability comes with time. Every mentor is different; some will warm up immediately, while others take longer to peel back the layers and reveal what makes them tick.

Another of my favorite mentors and trusted advisors is one of my professors from business school, Joel Peterson. He is currently the chairman of jetBlue and a beloved and esteemed leader at Stanford's Graduate School of Business as well as at the Hoover Institution. Joel is known globally for his leadership in communications, ethics, and values.

Whenever I have faced a fork in the road that involved any one of those areas, Joel has delivered sound advice. When I am not in a period of acute decision-making, I check in every six months to keep him informed about how my career is progressing. Most importantly, I let him know how his advice and perspective have impacted my career, as they invariably have for the better. That's **Leadership Hack 47 (Part 2): Be vocal about how your mentor has impacted your life—and thank them early and often.**

Ultimately, Joel's advice helped me decide when to exit a professional opportunity, while Christie's counsel helped me decide to take my current role as CEO. Sometimes it's not so much about specific advice as it is about having a wise and trusted sounding board to think through an opportunity in the context of one's career arc and long-term goals. I credit Joel with inspiring me to examine my value system and how it marries (or does not) with those of various business colleagues. I credit Christie with encouraging me to venture into new territory and new industries and stretch myself professionally.

> *No matter where you are in your career, the right mentor can energize you and provide counsel when you need it.*

No matter where you are in your career, the right mentor can energize you and provide counsel when you need it. And when you mentor others, you can accelerate their careers and help them succeed.

KICK-STARTING MENTEES' CAREERS

I am tremendously grateful for my own mentors, so it's no wonder I have found that being a mentor myself can provide great personal satisfaction. When you invest time and energy in someone, you not only change the trajectory of his or her life and career with your experience and wisdom, but your company or organization can reap rewards in the form of improved employee retention and job performance.

In my company, summer interns attend high-level team meetings to see firsthand how C-suite executives interact. I have brought interns to board meetings where they were able to observe and learn from confidential governance discussions.

I've talked about Anthony Overstreet, a brilliant young man and one of my Bulldogs on the Bay summer interns at Bottlenotes. When the summer ended, we extended his internship. Soon after, we made him a full-time offer, and just a few years later, he rose to director of operations. Anthony later joined me for a year as a partner at AJR Ventures before accepting a job at Facebook. I connected him with several opportunities that aligned with his interests along the way, including volunteering on a grassroots political campaign and joining Spark's Bay Area Advisory Board. To this day, I am glad I invested in him, and I admire his ongoing success.

Jinying Yang is another great example. What also started as a Bulldogs on the Bay summer internship evolved into a multiyear consultancy at each career phase: Bottlenotes, AJR Ventures, and even Surgical Solutions. In between, Jinying has asked if we could catch up so she could apprise me of her latest plans (join Lyft, leave Lyft to go to graduate school, get married, and more). She came to Chicago to visit for a day in transit from east to west to connect in person. She has done a perfect job of maintaining our relationship, so when a letter of reference or anything else is needed, she barely needs to ask, as the answer is, of course, yes. I feel connected to her life decisions and up-to-date on her whereabouts. Never are we catching up on lost time or ground. I also am deeply confident in her ability and would happily pull her into any future opportunity I could if only she were available. This is a mentorship relationship at its finest.

As an executive, I like to invest in talented people by offering them positions a half or full step above what they are expecting. Watching an employee grow into a new role is gratifying; boosting a person's sense of his or her capabilities often strengthens that person's loyalty to you and the company. When employees are challenged to learn and grow, they feel that management and mentors are invested in their success.

It isn't only up to the mentee to ensure the relationship thrives. A good mentorship is a two-way street, and there are a variety of hacks available to the mentor as well to help ensure success. ***Leadership Hack 48: Underscore that showing up matters.*** Lay out ground rules and expectations for your communications, establish parameters, set clear boundaries, and be direct with mentees regarding how often and in what communication method you hope to be contacted. Be clear about your availability in regard to both time and resources and what you can realistically offer and commit to.

Before you can offer suggestions or advice, you have to listen. ***Leadership Hack 49: Be an active listener.*** It may be tempting to jump in and solve things for your mentee, but they may not be asking for you to solve anything. Hear them out first. As you grow closer to your mentee, you may find that a part of you wants to protect mentees from falling on their faces. It's just like being a parent and not wanting your kids to make big, messy, painful mistakes. But sometimes you have to let them do exactly that. Your mentees will learn by trial and error. Sometimes the most valuable lesson you can teach your mentee is how to bounce back after a disappointment or setback.

Leadership Hack 50: Do what you say you're going to do. It's the golden rule of life as far as I'm concerned. If you say you will make an introduction, do it. If you say you will write a recommendation letter, do it. Whatever you say you will do, you must do. Period.

EMBRACING FEMINISM IN THE ERA OF MILLENNIALS

We can't have a conversation about mentorship without talking about the unique challenges and opportunities women face in today's world, both personally and professionally. No matter how you define your sex or gender, I urge you not to skip over this section, as it's an important conversation we need to have as a society, especially as we become increasingly polarized.

As evidenced by movements like #MeToo, women are creating powerful communities to both offer support and seek justice. After the US presidential election, millions of women around the world rallied together for the Women's March, which has become a January tradition since 2016. The word *feminist* has made a proud comeback, with various celebrities reclaiming the idea, everyone from superstar singer and producer Beyoncé Knowles to Emma Watson, the actress who played Hermione in the *Harry Potter* films and is now the UN Women Goodwill Ambassador fighting for gender equality.

As a female executive, entrepreneur, lecturer, wife, and mother of two little girls, I have a personal stake in this fight. Recent historical events have led me to think more deeply about my leadership style and desired impact. It leaves me hopeful of the change and leadership we women leaders are uniquely capable of driving in the world.

Nevertheless, we as women have not yet completed the last lap of the 26.2 miles required of our feminist marathon. We assumed that being a great team player was enough. It's not. We teach our daughters to be bold competitors, but professionally and politically, society is not yet ready for us to grab the brass ring we deserve. We are still living under a glass ceiling. Over half a century after the US government passed the Equal Pay Act, American women still face a substantial gender wage gap: at the time of writing this book in 2019, a woman working a full-time job earned 80.7 cents for every dollar earned by a man working full time.

Look at Geena Davis, a feminist pioneer for her work with See Jane, the Geena Davis Institute on Gender in Media. As their tagline states, "If she can see it, she can be it." *Decades* ahead of her time, decades before the #MeToo era, Geena Davis understood that "life will only imitate art" if at least 50 percent of the lead characters in television and film are women.

In other words: we *still* have an extraordinary amount of work to do to ensure that the feminist movement of the last seventy years doesn't rockslide backward in a matter of moments.

After the first year of the annual study being published, I discussed McKinsey's *Women in the Workplace* with my friend of twenty-five years, fellow Winnetka native, McKinsey partner, and fellow Stanford GSB alumna Alexis Krivkovich. Alexis distilled the state of the nation to me when summarizing the study's key takeaways:

Women fall behind early. If we don't support women being promoted *earlier* in their careers, the reality remains that very few women will be in roles that position them to become CEOs further down the line.

Women are at a disadvantage in their daily interactions because they see fewer women around them. Take a young woman who starts an entry-level position at a corporate law firm. She works with a full team of paralegals, legal receptionists, and law clerks, both male and female. But as you go further up the company hierarchy, there are fewer and fewer women, and all three partners in the firm are men.

This means that, as the new hire climbs the ranks, she'll lose her current community of female colleagues in the company—and she won't have any role models (or women mentors) to help shine a light on a potential future career.

The paradigm is not necessarily shifting dramatically enough to impact the millennial generation. Sure, we've all heard the sound bites. "More female executives than ever before!" "Women are getting hired at unprecedented rates!" While it is true that things have gotten better in many ways, progress has also stagnated in recent years. We're still facing large gender gaps, particularly at the top levels of leadership in government and business. The 2018 US midterm elections were groundbreaking: 117 women were elected or appointed to Congress, 102 to the House of Representatives and 15 to the Senate. These are heartening numbers—but it doesn't change the fact that women still only make up 23 percent of the House and 25 percent of the Senate, even though we account for almost 51 percent of the US population.[9]

That reality hits hard—and it's one we may not want to accept. Are we truly hearing the results of Alexis' McKinsey study? That even for our millennial generation, it will be more status quo, more glass ceilings, and fewer women in leadership? What can we do to accelerate a crucial shift?

Sheryl Sandberg, COO of Facebook and founder of Lean In, wisely calls on women in leadership positions and blooming careers to "lean in" to opportunities for growth and advancement. The wildfire-like global growth of her movement clearly demonstrates that this approach is a key solution.

---

9   Li Zhou, "How to Close the Massive Gender Gap in Congress," Vox, accessed August 20, 2019, https://www.vox.com/the-highlight/2019/8/7/20746147/congress-women-2019-gender-parity.

Perhaps given the state of today, we need to start leaping versus leaning. But how do we start?

Leadership Hack 51: Find someone to make you his or her protégé. This is a chapter about mentorships, so of course that's going to be my top suggestion. We professional women can build relationships via our university alma maters, at our offices, on our boards, and through formal and informal gatherings and organizations. Heck, we can even do so at children's birthday parties. Like the "consciousness raising" gatherings of the 1960s, we need to be conscious of the need to explicitly support our female peers, friends, and colleagues.

The most obvious way to do it is to let someone turn you into his or her protégé. Such a coach will inspire, guide, and support you by teeing up the proverbial springboards throughout your career. By providing introductions and opportunities that help you leap into your next venture, a great coach or mentor can help you soar to new heights that you might not have achieved without his or her catapult.

I'm lucky that my mother has always been a mentor and inspiration to me, both professionally and personally. She's also always had a tightly held group of women friends to lean on. Her choice in women friends has always inspired me—and sometimes those women have become my mentors. When I was given the opportunity to join Surgical Solutions, my mother's close friend Cherilyn Murer, whom she'd met on the University of Chicago Harris School Leadership Council, was endlessly gracious in her willingness to help me analyze the opportunity. She primed me on industry trends and helped me think through the potential upsides and potential pitfalls of this role at this point in my career. It was an absolute no-brainer to ask Sterling Partners, with whom Cherilyn already had an advisory relationship, to appoint Cherilyn to Surgical's board of directors, which they did. Cherilyn has proven a tremendous strategist and an unbelievable mentor and friend.

Leadership Hack 52: Support flexible work environments. The *Women in the Workplace* study states that "employees need the flexibility to fit work into their lives."[10] As a Silicon Valley CEO who dealt with four pregnant team members out of ten in a twelve-month period (one being me), I understood firsthand that providing flexibility can be a major challenge to an organization, particularly a small one.

However, I have found that women who are given flexibility are just as driven, resourceful, and dependable; if anything they overshoot that required mark in gratitude for the flexibility they were afforded. Providing one or two days a week of remote time for your trustworthy team members who are suffering from a grueling commute or allowing flexible hours to those with young children who need to take the early morning or midafternoon shuttle each day are examples of how to be flexible in today's work environment.

Leadership Hack 53: Do your absolute best to eradicate sexism in America's business environment. According to Ann Grimes, associate director of Stanford's Brown Institute for Media Innovation and former faculty fellow at the Clayman Institute for Gender Research, the good news is that we may have arrived at a "perfect storm" moment in the feminist movement as it relates to the millennial generation. When I sat down with Ann to discuss, she reflected:

> Something has shifted at Stanford. Young women are now willing to call themselves "feminists," whereas when I arrived on campus over a decade ago, they weren't. There appears to be a coalescing today similar to the women's

---

10   "Women in the Workplace—2018," McKinsey & Company, accessed August 19, 2019, https://womenintheworkplace.com/.

movement of the 1970s. It commenced with Title IX, which laid a foundation for a generation of girls—now young women—to compete on an even playing field as boys, especially in sports. Those young women now expect the same equality and equanimity in the workplace. It now seems we have a generation of women going into the workforce who would call themselves feminists.

If you're a man reading this, I'm talking to you, too. Insofar as feminism simply means women deserve equal rights as men, we should *all* be feminists.

If you agree with Grimes and consider yourself a feminist, what next? Spring to action. Whether you're marching, writing, speaking to a colleague who is demonstrating sexist behavior, call it out—clearly and succinctly. I'm going to borrow from Gandhi's considerable legacy of wisdom here for **Leadership Hack 54: "Be the change you wish to see in the world."**

It is incumbent upon women in leadership positions to capitalize on this "perfect storm" moment in the feminist movement. We have to embrace the feminists within: support ourselves, support each other, leap versus lean, and play to win.

CHAPTER 7

LEADING A TEAM: EVOLVING YOUR CULTURE

Hacks 55–64, Summarized

LEADERSHIP HACK 55

Stay packed with healthy snacks. It's easy (and cost effective) to keep wholesome food in the office: nuts, fruits, vegetables, popcorn, even quinoa. At Surgical we have water, tea, and coffee on hand, but no soda is allowed. By stocking up on nutritious food instead of cookies and candy, you'll help your team members keep a consistent energy throughout the day, hopefully avoiding afternoon burnout.

LEADERSHIP HACK 56

Find ways to make your team *want* to come to the office. For us it's DoorDash Mondays. For you it might be GrubHub hump days or casual dress Fridays. Put a little thought into what your team would respond well to. Frankly, I cast a strong vote for Mondays, since that's the most important day for people to come to work with a spring in their step.

LEADERSHIP HACK 57

Find ways to make your team want to *stay* in the office. This is an old Silicon Valley truism: If you can give them what they need, why would they ever need to leave? Hence the healthy snacks and beverages at Surgical, a Peloton, or whatever else you can think of to make your people comfortable and content. If they don't run out for coffee or take long lunch breaks, they'll be significantly more focused and efficient.

LEADERSHIP HACK 58

Make time. As a leader, it's your job to make time for your people. Walk-around management has always been important to me. And when there's geographical distance to contend with, we get on a video call. When people know you make time for them, their performance will be better, and you'll be more plugged in to what's going on with them on a personal and professional level.

LEADERSHIP HACK 59

Celebrate the wins. If you don't take time to celebrate the good stuff, you're losing a golden opportunity to connect with your team and to encourage them to connect with each other. You get to define how you celebrate in your company culture. Cupcakes? A toast? Starbucks gift cards? Whatever it is, make sure you're consistent. If you establish a precedent of emails on people's birthdays or work anniversaries, don't leave anyone out.

LEADERSHIP HACK 60

Invest in your people. Your team members are people, and people want to be believed in. It's basic human nature. We all have potential, and we want it to be acknowledged and nurtured by our colleagues and employers. Again, *how* you do so is up to you. If formal assessments are economically feasible, you might consider them. If not, you can find more innovative approaches, like I do by bringing in a star athletic coach like Abdul Sillah or The Wellness Executive, Eric Montes.

LEADERSHIP HACK 61

Give your people something of value—then observe how they receive it. Watching my team receive Abdul's athletic assessments was a powerful opportunity to see each of them as a unique human being, with strengths and areas for potential growth. What you're always looking for as a leader are fresh and different lenses through which to see your people so you can understand better how they work independently and inside the organization as a whole.

LEADERSHIP HACK 62

Do whatever you can to fast-track culture. There's something to be said for relationships maturing and strengthening over time. But you don't always have time, and when you're coming to a new company or organization, you want to do everything in your power to shore up the culture, especially if it's been lacking. Hacks I've found helpful in this regard include things like scavenger hunts, group workouts, team-building exercises and retreats, concerts, sporting events, and mini-massages. These are ways to forge strong bonds within your team in a relatively short amount of time.

LEADERSHIP HACK 63

Take a few minutes to connect as human beings before you get going.
Fight the urge to skip the pleasantries at the tops of calls or meetings so
you can get down to business. Instead, acknowledge that those "pleasantries" are a crucial way to begin. It's your job to know your people as
more than talking heads or suits sitting at desks. Check in with them.
Ask about their kids. If you connect on a human level first, the conversation will be more productive and harmonious on *all* levels.

LEADERSHIP HACK 64

Meet people where they are. If you demonstrate authentic leadership,
your team will feel like they can come to the table with their honest,
authentic selves too.

* * *

When Steven Taslitz tasked me with determining whether or not
there was a "*there* there" at Surgical Solutions, I realized I also needed
to take a hard, honest look at something close to home.

The corporate office.

The office culture at Surgical needed some work—not to mention
the office itself. I'd come straight from Silicon Valley, with its roomy
coworking spaces and open floor plans. In Chicago I walked into a
staid suburban office with fluorescent lighting and people scheduling
team meetings by text message. I felt like I'd time-warped back to 2002.

During my first sixty days—in the midst of going out on field
visits, assessing my people, and doing a deep dive to understand
industry trends—I was also implementing things like using Slack for
intrateam instant messaging and Dropbox for cloud-based file storage.

"Let's put some empowering words on the wall," I said. "We'll
change the floor plan a little and cluster desks so there are little hubs.

We're going to put out healthy food and snacks. Then we'll start a company newsletter and send out well wishes and/or inspirational quotes to people on their birthdays and on major holidays."

These actions might seem obvious—and *they are not hard to do.* A strong company culture makes *everybody* happier. No big shocker.

> A strong company culture makes everybody happier.

Surgical needed a cultural reboot.

Here's what I focused on to make it happen:

55. Stay packed with healthy snacks.

56. Find ways to make your team *want* to come to the office.

57. Find ways to make your team want to *stay* at the office.

58. Make time.

59. Celebrate the good times ... and the wins.

60. Invest in your people.

61. Give your people something of value—then observe how they receive it.

62. Do whatever you can to fast-track culture.

63. Take a few minutes to connect as human beings before you get going.

64. Be authentic.

FEED YOUR PEOPLE

The first thing to consider when rebooting a company's culture?

Snacks.

You can't talk about culture without talking about food. It sustains us, brings us together, and gives us a chance to interact with one another in a way that feels casual and authentic. This is why I invite my team over to my house to break bread—and it's why I think every office should be stocked with wholesome food.

Leadership Hack 55: Stay packed with healthy snacks. That's just common sense.

At Surgical, I make sure we always have coffee, tea, and water on hand. Soda is banned from the office, but healthy snacks are always welcome: nuts, fruit, popcorn, etc. We also do DoorDash Mondays, where everyone in corporate headquarters can order lunch on the house. The beauty of DoorDash Mondays is that people are relieved to start the week without having to pack a lunch.

Leadership Hack 56: Find ways to make your team want to come to the office. Food can provide an easy and effective path to doing just that. Which flows nicely into **Leadership Hack 57: Find ways to make your team want to stay at the office.** Having food around also keeps people there because they run out less, a good old tactic in Silicon Valley that applies to any office in the country. And of course some companies go further than that, treating their teams daily to breakfast or catered lunches.

At Surgical, DoorDash Mondays come with an added benefit: it gives *me* an opportunity to do a lunch and learn. I have a bad habit of scheduling phone meetings between 12:00 and 1:00 p.m., but whenever I'm not on a call, I try to take a ten-to-fifteen-minute break to get up, walk around the office, and talk to people. "How's the new puppy? Did your daughter win her hockey tournament? Are you looking forward to your vacation next week?" It's a chance to take the temperature of my team members and to connect with them on a human level.

Leadership Hack 58: Make time. I believe in walk-around management. It's old school, and it's what I learned from my stepfather during his macromanagement days at Chicago's East Bank Club. I can't do it every day, because sometimes I'm scheduled down to the fifteen-minute mark. But I'm continually finding ways to hack my own schedule. Maybe I carve out time to work on a deck, knowing that my patience level for that deck will be about thirty minutes, giving me another thirty minutes to walk around and talk to people. Or I don't schedule my first call until 9:30 a.m., giving myself thirty minutes at the beginning of the day to walk around, kibitz with people, and catch up at the watercooler or coffeemaker. The goal is to make time to have a real conversation that *doesn't* revolve around work.

Of course I also believe alcohol in moderation can be an effective team-building device. One of the most effective ways to get your people to open up is to offer them an end-of-day glass of wine every few months, when everyone pauses what they're doing to sit down and connect. At Surgical, I often tie this to something we're celebrating. I bring in a couple of nice bottles of wine and say, "Hey, it's four people's one-year anniversary with the company this week. Let's celebrate!"

Which brings us to *Leadership Hack 59: Celebrate the good times … and the wins.* At Surgical, our HR team makes note of everyone's birthdays, and I personally send out a happy birthday email to each employee. We celebrate wins and company anniversaries with a toast of something or some company swag.

This isn't rocket science. Feeding your people and nurturing your connections with them are such easy ways to vitalize—or *revitalize*—company culture. Why *not* orchestrate some fun, easy moments to celebrate the milestones, big and small?

INVEST IN YOUR PEOPLE

One of the mainstays of a thriving culture is *Leadership Hack 60: Invest in your people.* Assess their unique talents, and bring out the best in them.

There are formal and informal methods of assessment. People such as Andre Zafrani of Apogee Advisors will come in and assess a potential leader's (C-suite executive or board member) capability for the job and then pattern-match successes and failures in the past to predict the future. I've been on the other side of one of these: Sterling had me assessed before I took the job.

Knowing that an outside, third-party expert assessor had analyzed my strengths and weaknesses and had nonetheless recommended me for the role was encouraging, likely to both parties. The private-equity firm gained confidence that my life experience to date should set me up for success in the role, and I walked into the role with an extra boost of confidence, having been validated in that way. And the insights from the reports themselves can be exceptionally instructive and actionable.

While I wish we had the resources to do that kind of assessment with every one of my top executives, the reality is different. My hack for that has grown over the years into a bona fide strategy, one I find highly effective. At both Surgical and Bottlenotes, I developed innovative (and less expensive) ways to achieve similar results. *Leadership Hack 61: Give your people something of value—then observe how they receive it.*

Something I've done with every team I've ever run is to bring in Abdul Sillah to coach workouts. Abdul was been my fitness coach for over a decade and is a very dear friend; today, he's also an athletic agility coach to the stars. Abdul has trained everyone from Olympians to NFL players, professional baseball players, and professional tennis players. He coached Serena Williams and Sloane Stephens and currently works with Naomi Osaka, whom he trained when she was forty-second in the world ... and who is now number one.[11]

At Bottlenotes, I brought Abdul in to lead team workouts. Our team was naturally fit, men and women in their twenties and thirties, most of whom worked out already. At Surgical, I took a different approach. I had Abdul come in and do one-on-one athletic assessments and customized workouts for individuals. He conducted one-hour sessions with ten people, so I could give my team the gift of his expert time, attention, and advice that he uniquely has the talent to provide.

Abdul is an incredible agility and athletic coach, but really he's training the mind as much as the body with each of his clients. He's a psych undergrad, and I've found him to be exceptionally insightful about the psychology of human beings. Abdul is a very quick study on people. He has a real gift for distilling someone's psychological profile and physical makeup—and coming up with a bespoke set of recommendations.

After the sessions, I had an informal, unfettered, unfiltered conversation with Abdul about his experience with my people. There was no formal assessment or written feedback, but I got to talk to someone I deeply trust, hearing his character analysis after his one-on-one interactions with the team. Then I talked to my colleagues and heard *their* impressions of *him*. In other words, it provided a two-way feedback loop.

---

11   Reem Abulleil, "Meet the Fitness Coach Who Worked with Naomi Osaka, Sloane Stephens and Serena Williams: Abdul Sillah," Sport 360, accessed August 19, 2019, https://sport360.com/video/tennis/316556/meet-the-fitness-coach-who-won-the-us-open-with-naomi-osaka-sloane-stephens-and-serena-williams-abdul-sillah.

The athletic assessments were a way to invest in my people—to give them something of value—with a back-end benefit for me as CEO: it gave me a chance to assess them in a different environment. It wasn't a Rorschach or IQ test. I wasn't trying to trick anyone into revealing secrets about themselves I didn't know. But it did provide a way to see psychologically who had the propensity to quit and, conversely, who wanted to win and would try to win at all costs. Who was extra motivated? Who demonstrated unexpected determination while facing adversity? I witnessed how people coached one another and cheered one another on. It was an awesome character assessment—in a setting where everyone had sweaty good fun.

Within my first four months at Surgical, we also did an executive team and account manager team retreat. It included everything from sexual harassment training by our employment lawyer to big-picture visioning exercises. Then we launched a scavenger hunt organized by my HR team that sent team members all around Chicago. This proved to be a terrific way to get to know people while running around town doing something fun and exciting. Different people had a chance to employ their different skill sets while working in a team of four. Suddenly people had a shared language and funny stories (like the brand-new team member, now our director of employee engagement, who wore high heels to the point of blisters while running around in one-hundred-degree weather), a history that would have taken them months to build just sitting in an office.

Then, to celebrate my six-month mark at Surgical, I brought in a wellness executive: a massage therapist for pro athletes. Hal found him through a friend, and he's fabulous. Eric Montes has a corporate program, The Wellness Executive, in which he comes in to do half-hour diagnostics in a massage chair. I was inspired by something I'd seen in fancy Silicon Valley, where employees would pay twenty dollars for an hour-long massage and the company picked up the rest. What a great, morale-boosting way to keep team members well.

At Surgical we don't have a formal wellness program, so thirty-minute massages were my informal version. But again, investing in your people makes them happier, healthier, and more productive. After the massages, I heard my team saying things like: "Wow, my back feels much better" and "I didn't realize my posture had been so bad."

For me, these are all ways to give something to my team rather than just send them to a conference for outside training. In so doing, I am able to strengthen the bonds between team members while also setting up a fun, informal means of assessment. I save money while still giving them something of value. *Leadership Hack 62: Do whatever you can to fast-track culture.* Team-building exercises, workouts, scavenger hunts, retreats, tickets to a game, massages—whatever works for you.

REWARD YOUR HIGH PERFORMERS

It is no secret that the largest, most successful companies of all time have universally rewarded their top performers. Dedicating time to fast-track, recognize, call out, and otherwise build out a special path for high performers is crucial. My friend, entrepreneur and executive Scott Schrader, describes his program cogently and poignantly: "I have enrolled a select few of my talented folks to be part of an elite program that provides them with exposure to parts of the business that they would otherwise not have received. Yes, they are coming from the top US educational institutions. They would have left our company after two years for other opportunities unless I had showed, not told, them that they were part of the future. They became future leaders—transforming every piece of the business that they touched, and leaving those functions or divisions materially better—because of their love of the company/commitment to the bigger picture."

In short, Scott provides his elite performers with exposure to the upper echelons of management, the way the entire organization behaves—and as a result, they envision a leadership role for themselves in the firm and thus achieve it. ***Hack 62 (Part 2): Do whatever you can to fast-track culture*** … particularly incentivizing your top performers to *stay*.

HUMANIZE EVERY MEETING

We've talked about some of the big-picture ways to reboot and sustain a strong company culture. But culture also develops during the small, more mundane tasks.

For our weekly team meetings, we use video (Google Hangouts or Zoom), not just phone, where people can be doing other things. This is a spin-off of the "look them in the whites of their eyes" hack from chapter 4. Live virtual meetings help everyone feel present and like they're a part of the unit. We're all in the same boat, rowing to the same shore.

I always have weekly one-on-ones with my executive team. The scheduling can get jumbled because of complicated schedules, but it's important that we take the time. At the beginning we talk about our families or the big snowstorm that's coming—and then we naturally transition to work. That personal connection at the beginning is key. It's so obvious that it almost seems foolish to say, but it's amazing how many people forget ***Leadership Hack 63: Take a few minutes to connect as human beings before you get going.*** It will make the call much more productive if you take a little time to humanize the interaction first.

At Spark, one of the nonprofits on whose board I have served, we started with personal check-ins at the beginning of each call. It's really great to hear how people are doing. I wish we had time to do that on my weekly team calls at Surgical. I hope to bring it in at some point.

The most productive Monday meetings are when my key executives prepare agendas for our one-on-one sessions. Some have five bullets on them; one executive prepares a fourteen-point agenda and sends it to me in a Word document and crosses items off week over week. There's another executive who always has an agenda, written on an old-school notepad, but refuses to share it with me in advance of the meeting. I never know what I'm getting or what mood he'll be in. But it's always a productive conversation, and at the very least, well organized.

In short, my final leadership hack on culture: **_Leadership Hack 64: Be authentic._** And no matter what, buoy your people through the losses and troughs—and celebrate the wins. A little shared camaraderie goes a long, long way.

PART TWO: LIVE

Time is your most precious resource. Hack your time.

—Christopher Voss, founder and CEO of Black
Swan Group and author of *Never Split the Difference:
Negotiate as if Your Life Depended on It*

CHAPTER 8

THE BALANCING ACT: MOM, ATHLETE, ENTREPRENEUR, EXECUTIVE

Hacks 65–71, Summarized

LIFE HACK 65

You're not looking for daily balance. You're looking for episodic balance.
When people ask me, "How do you strike that perfect balance as a mom, wife, and businesswoman?" the answer is: I don't. Instead of daily balance, I strive for episodic balance, a concept I learned from one of my mentors, Joel Peterson (of Stanford/Hoover Institute/jetBlue fame).

LIFE HACK 66

Move your body, calm your mind. My morning workout sessions are sacred: I start every day on my treadmill or Peloton in my basement. If I work out, I quiet the chatter in my mind, and I can be truly present. Even if 6:00 a.m. workouts aren't your style, I encourage you to find other ways to move. It could be walking, yoga, cycling, HIIT classes—whatever gets you to that feel-good place in your body and in your mind.

LIFE HACK 67

Start strong, finish stronger. This one's self-evident. If you burn out halfway through the race, you're not going to finish it with as much grace, if at all. To quote my dear friend and athletic coach to the athletic stars, Abdul Sillah, "Start strong; finish stronger." Sure, you're going to need to course correct along the way. Said every athlete and parent everywhere!

LIFE HACK 68

Multitasking is not a choice; it's a necessity. If you're a parent who doesn't know how to multitask, learn quickly. This doesn't mean only being half present for your kids. It means finding ways to pair up tasks that work well together—engaging your kids in meal prep, talking to Grandma on the drive to school, etc.—and making your children active participants. Have open conversations with your kids about what they love and enjoy—such as crafts, reading, archery, sports, stories, nature—as a way of giving them ownership of the activities you do together.

LIFE HACK 69

You have to take care of yourself before you can take care of other people. Prioritize your own self-care. This will of course look different for different people: it might be an hour at the gym, a long walk, green juice, a hot bath, a good talk with a friend, an honest talk with a therapist. Only you know how best to take care of you. Just make sure you secure your own oxygen mask before helping others.

LIFE HACK 70

If you're on the verge of DEFCON 1, deploy diversionary tactics. This is a time-tested hack in our house. Sometimes the best way to defuse the bomb is to step away from the bomb entirely. With children, prior to a major explosion, divert their attention to something else—a book, a puzzle, a game, a video call with your spouse or coparent. These diversions can shift their emotional equilibrium before it goes completely off the rails. Same thing holds true for adults at a dinner party engaged in deep political discourse. I have seen evenings hinge on going off the rails over deep political divides. Instead, right before a moment gets too heated, bend the conversation to something related but different. Adults, too, can be diverted.

LIFE HACK 71

Invest in the level of flexibility that you can afford, both energetically and financially. Just make sure the system has slack. I remember my mom pioneering the childcare model in our home in the 1980s and early '90s with daytime help and a night-shift nurse who helped cover the childcare swing shift that those of us working moms know too well. Every family has to find the system that is emotionally, energetically, and financially feasible for them. But whatever you choose, make sure you've built in some slack.

* * *

I always knew I wanted to be a mother.

Perhaps it's because I'd grown up with a world-class mother myself. Former US Ambassador Fay Hartog-Levin (a.k.a. Madam Ambassador, a.k.a. MA, a.k.a. my mom) taught me many crucial life lessons, but perhaps paramount among them is this: family matters.

Showing up for family matters and building lifelong relationships with "friends who are family and family who are friends" matters.

My mother's youth was far from idyllic. While my grandfather's professional successes were storied and impressive, they lost my oma, Ada Menko, to stomach cancer when she was just fifty years old. My mother was only sixteen. My opa quickly remarried, and as the story was told to me, my mom was left to apply to college and get herself there on her own. She chose Northwestern—and to be a Russian major, no less, at the height of the Cold War. During her college years, in 1968, she traveled to Russia, where her passport was taken upon arrival with the "promise" of having it returned prior to departure. (Perhaps her later work with the State Department was preordained.) She graduated from Northwestern in three years and immediately set off for the Netherlands (where she got her first taste for going back to The Hague) and Austria to serve as a ski instructor.

Even back then, she had the resilience, self-reliance, and willingness to take the road less traveled, a trait that typified her life—and one that I suppose explicitly and implicitly shaped who I am from childhood to present.

My mom was a terrific role model. She showed and shows extraordinary dedication to her career, her health, and her closest friends. Throughout my life, my mother served as a big-firm attorney, an attorney for school districts, vice president of external affairs of Chicago's Field Museum of Natural History, a crisis-management strategist at Res Publica—all before becoming US ambassador to the Netherlands under President Obama. Having retired from that appointment, she is now a Weinberg Foundation trustee, a distinguished fellow at the Chicago Council of Public Affairs, an adjunct law professor, an advisor to many, and more.

In her commencement address to Northwestern University's Weinberg College of Arts and Sciences, she shared the keen insight that careers are not linear, yet in retrospect, all experiences build upon each other. Despite being a single mother for over five years of my life, she never stopped working toward what she wanted out of life. Her willingness to follow her heart, chase her dreams, and achieve the pinnacle of her own professional success inspired me tremendously—and continues to inspire me to this day.

As a mom, I wanted to be as inspiring and independent as my mother. And since I have the benefit of a partnership with my husband, I aspired to also be as fun loving and approachable with our children as possible (for which I give Hal more than half of the credit). I also knew I'd have the benefit of my mother's and my mother-in-law's love, support, and presence in our children's lives, an even larger gift.

I know how fortunate I am to have so many opportunities and avenues available to me as a parent. I want to be a mom whose children have a very rich and engaging relationship with their grandparents. I want to be a mom with a stellar husband who is also a loving, attentive dad. I want to be a mom who is inspiring yet present, who can do silly dance parties and snuggle up with her children in bed—and can also be free to lead a company and take a red-eye once a week as needed. I want to cook crepes for my family most mornings and go sledding on winter weekends, but I also want to sit on boards, write books, and do all the others things about which I feel passionate.

As I noted in the introduction, the concept of "doing it all" isn't just trite: it's impossible. There's no such thing. Not all at once, anyway.

Fortunately, I've found better wisdom elsewhere. The following hacks have led me through the many worlds I navigate—from the boardroom to the playroom—and unlocked a wealth of handy hacks along the way.

---

65. You're not looking for daily balance. You're looking for episodic balance.

66. Move your body; calm your mind.

67. Start strong; finish stronger.

68. Multitasking is not a choice; it's a necessity.

69. You have to take care of yourself before you can take care of other people.

70. If you're on the verge of DEFCON 1 (with your kids or even at an adult dinner party), deploy diversionary tactics.

71. Invest in the level of flexibility that you can afford, both energetically and financially. Just make sure the system has slack.

EPISODIC BALANCE

One of the best pieces of advice I've ever been given came from Joel Peterson, my mentor at Stanford Business School and the chairman of jetBlue, whom I talked about in chapter 6. I give Joel all the credit for **Life Hack 65: You're not looking for daily balance. You're looking for episodic balance.**

Here's what episodic balance means to me. There are going to be times I spend a lot of time with my husband and our kids and fill up that well with love and experience and connection. For example, we'll spend all of spring break together skiing, or we'll spend a week to ten days visiting friends around the country or elsewhere in the globe during the summer. During those times, my career takes a back seat. Work doesn't go away completely—it gets compressed like a toothpaste tube. I might push it down to an hour or two a day, knowing that it's time for me to fill the well as a mom and wife.

And then there are going to be many days where work takes the driver's seat. When I fly for work, which is often weekly, day trips are my favorite: 6:00 a.m. flight out to see a current or prospective client, and head right back. No matter if I am gone for one day or two (as I try desperately hard not to be away from our girls for more than one night in a given week, if any), when I'm on the road, I'm checking in with FaceTime and texts and getting photos from our childcare professional about how they are doing. But basically, for eighteen, twenty-four, or thirty-six hours, I'm not there. I have to trust that the infrastructure we've put in place—childcare, grandparents, after-school activities, etc.—is strong enough to hold. Hal and I always strive to be away at different times so the girls are never without both of us—but even so, three to five days a year, we are both gone at the same time. (The only silver lining is if and when, by the fates, we are away in the same place!)

Still, the fact that we've been able to work it out so at least one of us is with our girls, approximately 360 days a year—*that's* episodic balance. It's not daily, because I can't be with my kids all day, every day. Nor can Hal. Nor can I be at my job 24–7, 365 days a year. I strive to create balance in countless other ways, big and small, across the varied aspects of my life. I work to make sure the mom part of me is well tended, as are all the other parts.

This simple concept from Joel has been an essential building block of my parenting approach.

WORK IT OUT

Women in leadership positions are often asked how to maintain work-life balance. The more I have wrestled with this question over the years, the clearer I become about the answer. Spending time with my husband, daughters, siblings, parents, and close friends makes me happiest.

But there is only one answer to how I achieve balance: athletics.

Barring 6:00 a.m. flights or a sick nanny, I start my day at 5:00 or 6:00 a.m. with a forty-five-to-sixty-minute workout. It's not about vanity. It's about *sanity*. A daily workout helps me hit the reset button in my mind. It helps me burn off excess energy, anxiety, and accrued stress. More than anything, working out allows me to start each day with a clean slate.

I understand not everyone can work out every day. Much like "having it all," it just isn't possible. *You* get to define how and when to exercise. **Life Hack 66: Move your body; calm your mind.**

Don't take my word for it. There's a host of doctors, dieticians, athletes, and coaches who've spoken to the transformative power of exercise. It doesn't just help you physically; it helps you mentally and emotionally. For more than a decade from my late twenties to late thirties, I felt like I survived on a perpetual diet of endorphins, as an entrepreneur and CEO; working out calmed me down. Now as the CEO of a company with a host of responsibilities in addition to work, the endorphins continue to be of great benefit and fuel—but working out also revs me up.

I strive to push myself physically each day. Exercise is a crucial outlet for physical stress, but it also generates positive psychological spillover effects. Athletic activities are often about committing to a goal, believing in that goal, and shoving fear of failure out of your mind, committing instead to success. A winning attitude in athletics often translates to a winning attitude in all other areas of your life.

My mother has always been a brilliant example in terms of taking care of her own health. I have fond memories of entertaining my younger brother, Jeffrey, and myself in a kids' playroom at her aerobics studio, BodyWorks, on weekends in the late 1980s, replete with women in leg warmers and leotards over tights. My mom has religiously run or walked four to five miles every Sunday with a close friend for the past forty years.

Like many women, she has also battled BRCA-induced cancer— and she battled it with the resilience and stoicism she gained from coping with her own mother's death at sixteen. She said, "I am not dying from this. Period." She was right. My mom embraced the best of Western and Eastern medicine in her treatment and ultimate triumph over the indiscriminatingly awful disease that is cancer. Taking care of her physical health, her commitment to working out—all of these attributes undoubtedly shaped my own approach to challenges and hardships. I have no doubt my mother's winning attitude, in concert with great nutrition and modern medicine, saved her life.

A great example of why athletics can help reset the mind is a story about hurdles and sleds, taken from my own years of training with my friend and athletic coach, Abdul Sillah.

Track hurdles stand at thirty to thirty-six inches high, come up way above your waist at five-feet-six, and are frankly intimidating.

Picture this: Abdul tells you to jump over them without dancing (i.e., shifting from foot to foot before jumping).

For me, this rekindles my childhood fears ingrained by years of gymnastics. I stand there, realizing that these twelve consecutive hurdles are a choice, but *not* really a choice. *Am I going to let some physical obstacle get the best of my mind?* That's a common refrain of my inner voice. The real question is: Why don't I believe I can do it?

Then I do it.

"You survived," Abdul says dryly.

I do a little dance, shake off the nerves, and saddle up to the next hurdle.

"Survived again. Now let's pick up the pace."

The next week Abdul would raise the hurdles; I'd sweat it out, psyching myself up. Then out, then up again.

The irony is, I had it nailed. But even writing this now, I feel that small sense of physical doubt. And I know that it's the doubt, not the hurdle, that will get you each and every time.

Doubt is the hurdle. It will inevitably creep in. Acknowledge it; then send it on its merry way. If you don't learn to conquer your mind and conquer your fears, then self-doubt will be the cause of your demise. And if you cannot summon the true grit required to pull more weight than you thought you could bear, there's no point in walking up to the starting line. (See chapter 4, "Pivot versus Quit.")

This is why sleds are such an interesting contrast—particularly when saddled with a 140-pound human being. Sleds (not the Santa Claus variety, but the ones connected to nylon bands wrapped around your waist) don't intimidate me the same way hurdles do. Of course, after pulling them one hundred meters, you feel pangs of nausea. But sleds I've got nailed. They are about true grit: my specialty. They're about Velcroing the waistband, staring down the football field ahead without looking behind you to see how far you've come or how heavy the load is. You simply focus on putting one foot in front of the other.

The burn starts at the twenty-yard line. Badly. But that means there are only eighty yards to go. Then seventy. Then sixty. Before you know it, you're fighting for the last ten yards, out of gas. But it's only ten yards. I've often claimed that I can get through ten yards or ten seconds of anything.

Abdul is fond of reminding us all that it's not how well you start a race that matters, but how you finish it that determines champions. *Life Hack 67: Start strong; finish stronger.*

THE POWER OF MULTITASKING

Multitasking tends to get a bad rap. Psychologists say juggling more than one task at a time—especially more than one *complex* task—can not only take a toll on productivity but may even lead to catastrophic results.

My first response to that study is: Do those psychologists have children and full-time jobs? Because I am a big believer in *Life Hack 68: Multitasking is not a choice; it's a necessity.*

Real life is a series of sprints, whether they are short or long, the one-hundred-meter dash or the dreaded eight hundred. When you're running a company, there isn't any traditional downtime. That means I have to be smart and innovative about creating episodic balance.

I am with my kids every morning when not on the road. This is a sacred time, no work-related devices allowed. They color and draw while we make breakfast—and we get to be together. Some of my favorite time with my kids is my early time.

For me, multitasking does *not* mean writing an email for work while my kids are standing there trying to talk to me. That's a fail. Multitasking is showing them it's healthy for me to work out every morning. I try to do it before they wake up—but if they wake up and I'm in the basement, they are allowed to come down to the playroom and play or do YogaKids while I finish my treadmill sprints. If our girls wake up early enough, I'll ask them, "Do you want to work out too?" They have one-pound weights and their own minihurdles and other athletic gear so we can create their own obstacle courses. They also have a play kitchen, and sometimes they'll make me a pretend smoothie or tea that we "have" after I'm done stretching.

Another way to multitask is to enlist your kids' help, letting them invest as cocreators in the time you spend together. I like to do things with my girls that are fun and engaging, activities that give them a sense of inclusion and accomplishment. I say, "Help me beat the eggs for your crepes this morning," so they help me cook. We recently got a new puppy, so I might say, "Please play with Yoda while I make breakfast." Or we call Oma or Grandma on the way to school to say good morning.

Unless I'm out of town, I always try to drive my daughters to school myself. Whether we're talking about what's on the radio or what they're excited about doing at school that day or something that happened at school the day before, these conversations are the little connective tissue where you get a lot of interesting insights. Friends who have teenagers tell me that time is even more important as kids age. It's often the in-between hours where you hear the most.

I try very, very hard to take care of myself physically, emotionally, and mentally. That's a priority. Otherwise I'm not going to be the best mom, wife, CEO, board member, lecturer, etc. that I can be. It's like that hackneyed quote about securing your own oxygen mask first. *Life Hack 69: You have to take care of yourself before you can take care of other people.*

That said, being a parent does mean you'll have to give up some things you love. When I was pregnant with my first daughter, my dear friend and acclaimed venture capitalist Emily Melton said to me, "You have to give up something you love with each kid." I've found that to be true. I don't read for pleasure as much as I'd like. That ended when Audrey was born.

I loved to cook, but when my second daughter was born, I had to cut way back on cooking. I still cook on weekends when I can, and I love cooking breakfast with my kids. The simpler you can make things for yourself, the more likely you are to stick to them. I do waffles, crepes, and eggs well. Breakfast doesn't have to be a big production. It's really about sitting down with my daughters and sharing at least one meal a day with them. That's important to me.

However, my capacity as a cook swiftly diminishes as the day goes on. I just can't cook on weeknights anymore—I don't have the bandwidth. Enter Blue Apron, Plated, and a quick salad, most of which are usually prepared by the childcare professional before the girls are picked up from school.

There's a kind of freedom in realizing you don't have the bandwidth to do everything and eliminating some things. Every once in a while, Hal and I order our favorite Chinese food for dinner. Or if he's traveling, I might be bad one night and have apples, cheese, popcorn, and/or a glass of wine—and call it dinner. But at the end of the day, it just wasn't the best use of my time to set the expectation myself that in addition to being a wife, mom, and CEO, I would also have to cook for us all a hot, healthy dinner and put it on the table every night.

The challenge, of course, comes when I'm exhausted or depleted. I won't lie to you: sometimes it's a struggle to not let professional stressors spill over into our home life, or vice versa. We are human beings, not robots. And there will be times when your kids are being extremely antagonistic and difficult. That's what kids do. Maintaining patience is hard when my daughters are fighting with each other and I'm thinking, "Come on. We only get a limited amount of time together every day. Let's make the most of it."

The best hack I've come up with in terms of defraying conflict is distraction. ***Life Hack 70: If you're on the verge of DEFCON 1, deploy diversionary tactics.*** This hack has evolved from life as a parent and as an attendee of dinner parties with politically charged discourse.

For example, in our home, if Henriette wants to read story A, but Audrey starts getting upset because she really wants to read story B, I'll often present a third option: story C. This is a helpful way of diverting a meltdown before it happens. Or now that we have Yoda the bernedoodle, I might divert by saying, "Let's play with the puppy!" Once in a while, the diversion works to diffuse the child bomb (i.e., tantrum). At the end of the day, I do my absolute best to be as positive and loving as I can be. I love my kids with all my heart. That part isn't hard. But keeping one's cool in the heat of sibling civil war? Harder. Diversions often help.

The same holds true at adult dinner parties with politically charged viewpoints. Usually in every dinner party larger than six with well-educated, passionate people in attendance, there comes a conflict between a limousine liberal and a political centrist. I have seen more than one evening almost devolve into meltdown (someone standing up and walking out, a host or hostess feeling deeply offended by a guest's behavior, etc.). In the perfect world, we would all always behave as if we were in an academic setting, keeping political discourse intellectual and not emotional, attacking the idea not the person. But back on the ranch, that rarely proves true. Finding a way to bend a conversation to a related but different topic right before a political landmine explodes is often a way to preserve the tenor of an evening and avoid DEFCON 1 in the same way one does with children. Diversions often, although not always, work.

SLACK: NOT JUST IN THE CLOUD

I have friends whose kids have slept methodically and flawlessly since they were two months old because they were so scheduled. I understand how to do that with a dog but not with a human.

I've always said I'm a slave to a routine, not a schedule. I have my morning time with Audrey and Hettie and take them to school, and then the childcare provider picks them up while I'm at work. They have their snack and then go to their afternoon activities; once they're home, they have some free choice time and then dinner and then a bath. I either give them the bath, or I'm back at the tail end of the bath. Then we lay out two to three books, depending upon length and energy levels, and share our daily Peaks and Pits, something I learned from my friend Marissa Mayer. Marissa and I have children who are around the same age, and I was inspired when she told me about doing Peaks and Pits with her kids at the end of the day. I adopted the idea to use with my daughters. Peaks and Pits gives them an opportunity to say what the high point of their day was and what the low point was—and for me to hear it.

After Peaks and Pits, we sing "The Sun Will Come Out Tomorrow," and I tuck them into bed. Whether bedtime happens at 7:55 or 8:25 p.m. doesn't matter, because if I stuck that closely to a schedule, I'd lose my mind. My life—as well as the lives of other working moms I know—just doesn't have that level of rigidity. It requires more flexibility. Sometimes things happen a half hour earlier, sometimes an hour later. It's a routine, not a schedule. That's the system that works for us.

For you, your ideal system might be different. I have friends who decline dinner events—or who don't take the last work call—so they can be home to put their kids to bed with military precision. Their children are more routinized than ours, but they're also less nimble. So there's a plus and a minus, a blessing and curse. It's really just a choice.

The one unassailable truth is that the system needs slack. It is hard to be solely dependent on one childcare provider, because people get sick and emergencies come up—and then your whole life goes sideways. You need slack for emergencies and unexpected things, and then you also need coverage for slack in your professional and social lives.

Case in point: I still want to be able to have dinner alone (a.k.a. date night) with my husband every several weeks. That means we need someone who can watch our kids at night, sometimes at the last minute. For now, that means having childcare professionals who split the duties and shifts. When our daughters are a little older, we'll likely lean even more on grandparents or family friends.

In my experience, to have adequate slack in terms of childcare, you either need professionals who split shifts or a spouse who stays at home, works from home, or has flexibility in his or her job. Or you need grandparents, close friends, neighbors who live nearby—people you trust with your kids.

I have girlfriends who've had great experiences with online destinations to source childcare providers. Others are fine with the high schooler next door as the afternoon babysitter—and others use formal agencies to recruit and vet their childcare professionals. Today there are great sources for finding credited, screened, background-checked people to come work with your kids. I have some friends who organize wonderful nanny-share arrangements with other families; other friends have one nanny per child. I have friends who have one nanny, and they find the other twelve to fifteen hours of weekly slack with grandparents/family. I have friends who have three children in daycare, which is collectively more expensive than one nanny alone but still their preferred path forward. I have friends who decided that for the first five years of their child's life, one of the spouses would off-ramp just to shuttle people around and then jump back in once their son or daughter started kindergarten.

The point is that there's no one model that works. The trick is *Life Hack 71: Invest in the level of flexibility that you can afford, both energetically and financially.* Just make sure the system has slack.

And most of all, to quote Joel Peterson's "last lecture" during our final year of business school: know what the big rocks are in your life. In short, prioritize the people who matter most to you and cherish them. Honor them. Do your best to put them first—after yourself— over and above any of life's baloney. If you know who matters most to you and why, your life choices in many ways define themselves.

CHAPTER 9

CELEBRATE GOOD TIMES (COME ON!): WORK HARD, PLAY HARD

Hacks 72–77, Summarized

LIFE HACK 72

Work hard, play hard—and work out afterward. 'Nuff said.

LIFE HACK 73

If you feel beautiful, you are beautiful. Since I don't get my hair and makeup done often, I feel beautiful when I do. But I also feel beautiful when I'm doing something that makes me feel powerful and strong. True beauty can happen when you're covered in sweat just as easily as when you're covered in sequins. What's important is that if you *feel* beautiful— then you are.

LIFE HACK 74

As long as you know the rules, they can be broken. This applies to all areas of life, not just throwing a good party. Learn the rules, know *why* they work, and then, once you've achieved a certain level of competence, trust your own instincts on how best to break them.

LIFE HACK 75

No matter what kind of event you're hosting, thoughtfully curate your seating arrangements. Then carve out a little time to visit with each guest. This hack has served me well time and again. If you take the time to think about where people are sitting—and to connect with them one-on-one—they will feel appreciated for attending an event. Do what you can to be generous to your guests. A big part of the joy of celebration is being able to give to your family and friends.

LIFE HACK 76

Build in enough flexibility that your guests can create their own experiences. Don't micromanage your events. Plan and curate them well, and make sure there is always good food and drink available—that part's non-negotiable. Also give your guests space to breathe. Build in opportunities for them to make their own meaningful experiences within the given context.

LIFE HACK 77

Sometimes people need an excuse to have fun. Your job is to give it. We all live busy, stressful lives. Sometimes all we need to kick back and let loose is permission. This is one of the best gifts you can give your guests: an invitation to have a great time. Whether you're throwing a birthday bash, family reunion, holiday party, retirement celebration—any event, really—never hesitate to be the arbiter of fun.

* * *

My younger brother, Jeff, and I grew up in a family where birthdays were a big deal. For years our mother celebrated her milestone birthdays in inventive ways: one year she invited her girlfriends to celebrate from the first row of a James Taylor concert at the Ravinia Festival, the oldest outdoor musical festival in the United States. For her sixtieth, we grabbed our hiking boots and ascended Aspen Mountain so she could capture a family photo showing us all "high on [her turning] sixty." For her seventieth, she took seventy of her closest friends and family members out for dinner, drinks, and a curated architectural tour on the Chicago River to "sail into her seventies."

In many ways, I am my mother's daughter. For my thirtieth birthday, Hal and I enjoyed a trip to Burgundy with our dear friends, and I hiked Mount Kilimanjaro with my brother, Jeff, the best hiking partner—and one of my best friends—in the world.

And then it was time for the big four-oh.

I wasn't dreading forty. We had just moved back to Chicago. I have a husband I deeply love and two children whom I love to the moon and back, and I am in the midst of an exciting and challenging phase of my career amid my Surgical Solutions journey.

Although our nuclear family was blessedly healthy and happy, life was happening all around us. Some of our very dearest friends were battling cancer, organ transplants, and publicly announced childhood traumas.

In spite of these dichotomies—or perhaps because of them—I knew I wanted to take a page out of Fay Hartog-Levin's birthday playbook and curate an unforgettable experience to usher in my fifth decade around the sun. I wanted to celebrate what we had and make the most of every moment because life can change in an instant.

In the last chapter, I talked about balance. For me, a big part of balance means living a full life. I find the comment "How do you do it all?" shallow and inaccurate. I think the comment I have heard that I admire the most—and hope to live up to myself—is "Wow, they live a very *full* life." The only way to do so is by *choosing* to live a full life. It's about being present in the moment. You can work yourself to the bone, but if you never take time to celebrate the good times, let alone kick back, then you're missing the point.

I've always been a big believer in "work hard, play hard." (And I think my younger brother, Jeff, can credit me for instilling the value in him, although he probably does it even better than I.) My fortieth birthday celebration was a testament to the latter half of that adage. Because the thing about playing hard is, it *isn't* all that hard—if you can hack it.

72. Work hard, play hard—and work out afterward.

73. If you feel beautiful, you are beautiful.

74. As long as you know the rules, they can be broken.

75. No matter what kind of event you're hosting, thoughtfully curate your seating arrangements. Then carve out a little time to visit with each guest.

76. Build in enough flexibility that your guests can create their own experiences.

77. Sometimes people need an excuse to have fun. Your job is to provide it.

EMILY POST GOES TO VEGAS

As a Silicon Valley entrepreneur, I witnessed some incredible fortieth birthday extravaganzas. I had billionaire friends who rang in forty by putting forty friends on a private jet and flying them someplace exotic.

With forty looming, I didn't have the means to do quite that.

Las Vegas is a fascinating place—and, by so many measures, "not me." I don't gamble, for one. But I do love the restaurants, the shows, limited amounts of time under the sun, and the 100 percent laissez-faire, nonjudgmental atmosphere. Plus, I had a great track record in Vegas: Jeffrey Rapp's twenty-first that I hosted was The Hangover before *The Hangover*—but that is his story to tell, not mine. Also, my bachelorette party in Las Vegas was filled with my most fun girl and gay male friends, an epic extravaganza that may never be exceeded (thank you to all those who participated).

With forty fast approaching, Hal and I put on our thinking caps and asked: What would feel right and fun for *us*? We ultimately decided to invite a bunch of people we loved to Las Vegas for my birthday weekend. We left our kids with my parents so we could enjoy uninterrupted time together and with our friends. Sometimes you just need to be a kid again.

We invited thirty-five people, assuring them that, if they got themselves to Vegas, we'd take care of the rest. We figured we'd have a turnout of around half. We were wrong—almost *everyone* said yes. I was one of the last people in our peer group to hit the milestone birthday, so I guess it was everyone's last opportunity to let the good times roll in the name of forty.

On Friday night we had a small, intimate dinner with my family members and any friends who'd come from overseas. We figured, if you came all that way, you deserved an extra meal.

Then Jeff delivered my one birthday request: to dance into the next decade. Everyone met us at his chosen club for a few timeless hours to dance on the proverbial tables, for old times' sake. The theme was "Dancing into the Next Decade."

On Saturday, I forced some of my Yale gal pals to work out with me at 8:00 a.m. with one of our girlfriends who used to be a trainer for the rich and famous. I wasn't seeing stars that morning; I was just tired. But as is always the case, I felt better after I sweat a little. *Life Hack 72: Work hard, play hard—and work out afterward.*

Most attendees lounged by the pool much of the afternoon— and some friends who had traveled in with their children enjoyed the best of Vegas that is family friendly. My sister-in-law Amanda graciously took me to get my hair done. I can't for the life of me do hair and makeup myself—I don't have the talent—but I look far better when it's done. *Life Hack 73: If you feel beautiful, you are beautiful.*

In the Dutch tradition, there's singing at all major life events, and the songs often bring in personal details of someone's life. There were personalized songs for my mom's "Sailing into Seventies" party, Hal's and my wedding, Jeff and Amanda's wedding, and many cousins' weddings in between. In that tradition, one of my lifelong best friends from college, Ben Eakeley, gave a special a cappella performance of "There's Only Us," an homage to Anthony Rapp's *Rent*, and a toast to me, at the evening's kickoff festivities. Those festivities included a champagne toast generously provided by one guest (no life event would ever be the same without you, Sydney!), handmade truffles by another attendee (you're one of a kind, Amy!), and a champagne sabering demonstration (love you, Baumgarten family!). There was not a dry eye in the room.

Thereafter, the party officially kicked off. Here's a little-known secret: if there's a food and beverage minimum for a space and you agree to meet it, you can often ask to send in your own wine and have corkage waived. Since we met the minimum, they let us pour a special wine for my birthday: the Henriette red blend Hal and I created, which we'd named after our daughter Hettie. That meant we didn't have to pay the obscene corkage fee on our wine. We also weren't overpaying for the wine itself, so we got more bang for our buck on that capstone event.

Some have called this book *The 4-Hour Workweek* meets Emily Post. Emily Post is iconic, the wellspring of all appropriate decorum around entertaining, including notions like "never seat couples together" and "always seat guests boy, girl, boy, girl." I actually think there's a lot of wisdom to that, if you're planning a White House or a state dinner. And whenever I host a dinner party in my own home, I often observe that as a general rule. But for my birthday, I was an ardent devotee to *Life Hack 74: As long as you know the rules, they can be broken.* In other words: once you know and value the basics, you can be contemporaneous.

With smaller table arrangements of fours and sixes, I paired people who either hadn't seen each other in a long time but knew each other, or were in affiliate industries, or had never met but were very close to me for different reasons. For example, I paired my childhood best friend, Amanda, a surgeon, with my friend who is also my personal doctor. They were the same age with similar educations, and I knew they'd have a lot to talk about, even though they'd never met. I also broke the rules and sat couples together.

I had a lot of fun playing with the seating arrangements. I even created a PowerPoint slide where I could move people and tables around, trying out different combinations. It was important to me that I think about my guests' experiences in addition to my own. We also created handwritten name cards, because why not? *Life Hack 75: No matter what kind of event you're hosting, thoughtfully curate your seating arrangements.* I find that people invest more in getting to know their table mates if they feel you have thoughtfully sat them in that seat for a specific reason.

It was fun to have people of all ages, from thirties to sixties, eating, drinking, and dancing together. There were friends I see every day and others I hadn't seen in ages, from work and home and various stages of my life.

The best advice I got all weekend was from my husband. After dancing all night and dining for three hours, I said, "What are we going to do next? We should all go to a show!" To which Hal gently replied, "Or maybe at midnight we're *not* going to over-schedule everyone, and they can just do their own thing." That was the right advice—particularly as Hal closed the dinner event with a toast around midnight, which was my most heartfelt moment of the weekend.

I tend to be overscheduled versus underscheduled, which is why I'm grateful to Hal for reminding me to add back downtime. It's a great *Life Hack 76: Build in enough flexibility that your guests can create their own experiences.*

After dinner, attendees were left to choose their own kind of fun. Ten of us went dancing for an hour and called it a night, ten other people went gambling, and fifteen others went to sleep. It was a perfect, organic end to the evening.

That's something else I've learned from throwing parties. *Life Hack 77: Sometimes people need an excuse to have fun.* Your job is to give it.

THE MORNING AFTER

I've learned a few things as I've aged, and one of them is how to be more responsible about how I treat my body. Whenever I take a red-eye, for example, I eat perfectly and don't drink any wine for a couple of days, since the flight is hard enough on me. I don't drink hard alcohol. I try very hard to avoid desserts. But make no mistake: there was no piety in Las Vegas. We had plenty of wine. But for my birthday weekend, I shut down all drinking at midnight.

As such, the next morning, I was able to informally "hold court," where anyone could swing by for a cup of coffee and goodbyes if they wanted. We chose to commemorate the occasion with ridiculously tacky but amusing fortieth birthday T-shirts, and I also gave each room a bottle of Henriette's wine to say thank you for coming.

My philosophy on parties and events is that your guests are giving you something by attending, so give them something in return. My friends were generous to spend the time and resources to get themselves to Vegas, so I wanted to shower them with gratitude and spoil them with fun. This was my gift to myself.

When I say work hard, play hard, I'm not implying that all of life is footloose and fancy-free. I'm also not saying I do it perfectly or that I've got it all figured out. I'm saying you can have a four-hour dinner with people you love and go dancing until two in the morning and still be gunning to go to work on Monday. You can party hard in Vegas Friday through Saturday—and still be excited to pick up your kids on Sunday.

It's all about how you decide to strike the right balance between work and play. It won't be the same for you as it is for me. But that's what's great about it. *You* get to choose.

CHAPTER 10

SOMETIMES IT'S THE LITTLE THINGS: TWENTY-THREE MINI-HACKS YOU NEVER KNEW YOU NEEDED

My goal in writing this book has been to share some of the hacks that have been most meaningful to me, ways of thinking, doing, and being that have shaped my path as an entrepreneur, CEO, wife, and mother.

Of course, there are some hacks that don't fall neatly into these overarching categories. As I was strategizing and structuring this book, I discovered a number of hacks I'd developed for dealing with the incidentals. And, as we all know, the incidentals often make up the majority of our days.

Think of this chapter as your handy pack of hacks, ones you can pull out on various occasions, whether you've just bought a new puppy or need a healthy go-to snack. Below you'll find hacks for kids, partners, dual-career households, bodies, technology—and quinoa.

Hacks for Kids

LIFE HACK 78

Day trips are your friends as a working mom. I don't like to be away from my kids for more than one night, so I try to schedule day trips whenever I can. In December, I often fly to Los Angeles for eighteen hours to attend the American Ballet Theatre's holiday gala. It is a great excuse to see some of my most beloved LA girlfriends and support the ABT, an organization about which I feel passionately, largely because of their dynamo executive director, Kara Medoff Barnett. Instead of spending the night at the hotel, I am on a red-eye back to Chicago by 11:00 p.m. so I can take my girls to school the next morning.

LIFE HACK 79

Read to your children before bedtime. Bedtime reading is one of my greatest quiet times with my daughters. It forces me to be present. It's a timeless, age-old parenting tip—and it's been around so long for a reason. I try to let each girl pick a book, and then we read together. Of course, as your little ones become readers, they can also read to you. Now that Audrey is reading, we sometimes swap pages: I read a little, and then she does. Bonus perk: it's a nice way for me to assess how her reading skills and reading comprehension are coming along.

LIFE HACK 80

Maximize your quality time with your children. In my family, that means doing crafts, coloring, playing, cooking, and talking early in the morning. Curated crafts and science experiments are truly awesome for inventive, prepackaged, premeasured activities (our early-childhood favorites today are Kiwi Crates and Little Passports). A periscope? Check. Homemade soapmaking? Check. Protect that time and energy, so you can treasure the quality moments with your kids.

LIFE HACK 81

Don't sugarcoat. We live in strange times. There's a lot of upsetting stuff in the news, from school shootings to political unrest. Some people try to completely shelter their children from the unpleasant realities, and that approach might work for you. For me personally, I've found the best policy is to tell the truth but in children's terms. I am fiercely committed to protecting my children. But you can't protect them from the truth; you can only present it in a way that makes them feel safe and supported. When they see something and ask about it, I try to be honest about what's happening in the world, in a way they can understand without feeling destabilized and afraid. If a child at school is mean or bullying them, I acknowledge the pain, reinforce over and over again that Hal and I have their backs, and remind them that when people are mean, walk away. They're not worth your time.

LIFE HACK 82

If your child throws a tantrum, record it. This is Hal's hack, but it's a great one, so I'm including it. When one of our daughters throws a tantrum, he'll record a video of it on his phone. The second he starts showing it back to them, they quiet down immediately. Sometimes all your children need to get a handle on their own emotional outbursts is a reminder of how those outbursts look from the outside. To be clear: I'm not suggesting you shame your children, but sometimes the sight of oneself midtantrum is so shocking, it can quickly silence even the most outraged toddler. (I know, you're thinking: "Would that work on adults too?" Do share!)

Hacks for Partners

LIFE HACK 83

Write love letters. I write my husband love letters every year on our anniversary and on Valentine's Day. And I mean proper love letters, not just rapidly scrawled Post-it notes. Hal wrote me one for our anniversary a few years ago that I carry in my purse. Just looking at the envelope in which it sits makes me smile. When our children are a little older, I'll do the same for them. This is a beautiful and authentic way to shower people with praise and remind them of all the things you love about them.

LIFE HACK 84

Make time to go out with your partner, just the two of you. Because we have intense and complicated schedules, I cherish our alone time. I recently said to my mother-in-law, "The more time I spend with Hal, the more I think, 'I wish we had more time together, just us.'" As crazy as our lives get, it's important to me to carve out date nights where we get to be husband and wife *without* our children tagging along. Cherish your time with your whole family, but make sure you're investing in your partnership one-on-one too.

Hacks for Dual-Career Households

LIFE HACK 85

Try not to both be away at the same time. Hal and I have been married for almost a decade, and I can count on one hand the number of nights a year we're both away from our kids. Do what you can to establish consistency at home, and work with each other to make sure you're coordinating for everyone's benefit.

LIFE HACK 86

Help your partner help him or herself. Hal and I both understand how important it is to each of us to work out. It's our most dependable slice of sanity. On Sunday mornings, for example, Hal lets me go run with our dog or lift weights with a friend; later in the day, I know he needs to go swim, so I take the girls. For you or your partner, it might not be working out, but there will inevitably be things you both need to stay healthy and sane. Find ways to support each other in those endeavors, and coordinate your schedules so that you can each do those things that you need to do for *you*.

LIFE HACK 87

Leverage your partner's strengths. Hal and I bring different strengths to the table: he's calmer, wiser, and less flappable than I. He's an excellent parent—especially under duress. I'm better at the routine. I know children need it. The point is: parenting is a team sport. Make sure you're working together.

Hacks for Body

LIFE HACK 88

To survive a red-eye, follow these four tips: 1) hydrate like hell, 2) eat crazy clean for the following two days, 3) power through until your kids' bedtime the next day (no naps), and 4) work out, but not too hard. Take it from someone who takes too many red-eyes: these four things are absolutely essential. I drink a ton of water and no alcohol. I eat extremely cleanly, including what I imbibe; these days I'm doing apple cider vinegar, green juices with ginger, and homemade organic bone broth or veggie broth so I can load up on nutrients. I don't nap, because I know if I can power through the day, I'll sleep soundly that night. And while I love to work out hard, on red-eye mornings I choose a lighter intensity exercise to get the blood pumping without exhausting myself. If you get too depleted, you'll get sick.

LIFE HACK 89

Respect thy body. My mom gets all the credit for this one. Before I went to Yale, she took me on a walk around the neighborhood and said, "Your body is not a wasteland. You only get one, so do right by it. Take care of yourself." It's some of the best advice I've ever gotten. I plan to pass it on to our children.

Hacks for Technology

LIFE HACK 90

Use your time wisely at thirty thousand feet. One of the biggest perks to having a laptop is that you can work from anywhere—yet there are precious few places where you can crank down the volume of life's other distractions to truly focus on the task at hand. Airplanes are one of those places. I edited a good portion of this book on flights to and from Chicago. Treat every flight like a gift, a sacred sliver of time when nothing can interrupt you.

LIFE HACK 91

Limit your children's screen time. In our family, we have found that iPads are a tool for addiction. They have a way of morphing the brain and creating withdrawal symptoms when you turn them off. When our daughters' school imposed a recommended screen break, we found that their behavior was so much better, we made it a house policy to nuke iPads unless we are traveling. The girls are allowed end-of-week movie nights on Fridays, and we are pretty liberal with educational shows Saturday mornings and Sunday nights. If they haven't been watching shows on a weekend, I'll sometimes let them play educational games on their iPads like Osmo, which has a number of educational games designed around coding, math, coloring—you name it. The benefit of restricting screen time is that a) when they do get it, they appreciate it more; b) it can be used for special occasions, like when traveling on a plane and you need your kids to go comatose with headphones on; and c) it means we get to devote our morning time to coloring with crayons and paper—no devices allowed.

LIFE HACK 92

Write handwritten thank-you notes. As we move into this digital age of depersonalization, it can be powerful to go back to the basics. Technology is amazing because it accelerates the rate at which we can interact, but it doesn't supersede the need to build meaningful relationships—and one of the best ways to do that is by writing. Every year I ask my children to handwrite thank-you notes to their teachers—and I do the same—to cultivate and nurture those relationships. I also write thank-you notes to close friends, family, mentors: for a special lunch date, for sending me flowers to acknowledge an important life event, you name it. When writing acknowledgment notes to team members, I strive to name specific traits and talents I admire most in each of them. I always acknowledge people's birthdays, and I try to send them a handwritten card, if not an email or text acknowledgment. When someone at the office does something extraordinary, I might unexpectedly give them a $25 gift card to say congrats on a job well done. Amazingly, handwritten and in-person acknowledgment in the digital age inspires surprise and delight. Of course there are times when life just gets too hectic and I have to make do with an email. But whenever possible, I strongly suggest you write notes by hand. Emails just don't have the same personal touch.

LIFE HACK 93

Tape your favorite quote to the bottom of your laptop. That way, every time you pack up your laptop, you'll see it and feel inspired. Mine is from my friend Jacki Rigoni, world-class copywriter and marketer: "You are one decision away from the life you want." To me, this means that every day is an opportunity to make a small decision to live your best life.

Hacks for Scheduling

LIFE HACK 94

Schedule everything. My team always laughs at me, but I have to schedule every. Single. Thing. My Outlook/Google calendar is my North Star. I'm a visual learner, which means if I don't see something on a page or on a screen—and if I don't get it down in writing right away—my brain might not store it. My calendar works retroactively too: I might not remember what I had to do, but if I see that I talked to you on Monday, then I can remember what we talked about. It's also a way for me to remember from a cadence standpoint: my calendar records how often I've had touch points with people I need to be in touch with. If I have a phone or video meeting, I need to have the call-in number or the Google Hangout link in my calendar; if it's an in-person meeting, I need the address of where I'm driving. I don't build in time, nor do I have an entire support team (just one superstar chief of staff, Irina—thank you for all that you do!), at this point in my life to do the prevetting to track down the number I'm calling or where I'm going. The Outlook/Google calendar dictates all.

Hacks for Emails

LIFE HACK 95

Stay on top of emails. We all know how emails pile up very quickly, making it hard to stay on top of your inbox. If I can answer an email immediately and efficiently—if it doesn't require a long response—I fire off a reply. Then I can clear it off the top of the queue. The other perk to responding with lightning speed is that the recipient feels acknowledged and appreciated. Sometimes, if you tackle the small stuff first, you will be better able to schedule the big, meaty stuff, reserving the majority of your energy for those big rocks.

LIFE HACK 96

It's fine to write angry emails—just don't send them yet. I have drafted some flagrantly angry emails in my day. It helps me blow off steam, and frankly, sometimes they're warranted. The hack is: don't send them—at least not if you're still angry. When writing an emotionally incensed email, put your own name in the "to" field, and save the draft for one to five days before you determine whether it should be sent, edited, or deleted. Part of the point was just putting it on paper. It's like a miniexorcism: you've gotten your anger out in words and given those words time to breathe; now you can rationally decide the best course of action.

Hacks for Hosting

LIFE HACK 97

When hosting an event at your home, create ways for your children to help prep. Whenever we have a dinner party, the girls help make place cards for each person. Of course the cards are adorable, so guests love them. But on the flip side, it gives my daughters an excuse to practice their penmanship—and it gives me a way to share with them who's coming into our home. That matters to me. For you and your family, it might not be place cards; maybe you invite your children to help you prepare the meal or plan another aspect of the party. The goal is to help your kids feel ownership of the event.

LIFE HACK 98

Whenever you can host an out-of-town colleague at your home, do so. Having colleagues stay at your house enables you to have the in-between moments to connect, which doesn't happen if they're off at a hotel. Your colleague sees you in your home environment, so they get to know you that much better. They also get to know your spouse and children. This affords you the opportunity to have the natural conversations that grow out of being able to sit down for a cup of tea or glass of wine at someone's kitchen counter. It's simply more efficient and organic.

LIFE HACK 99

Invite parents to your kid's birthday parties—and make it worth their while. Normally birthday parties are a cringing experience. When we lived in Silicon Valley, some of my closest girlfriends would have Bloody Mary bars or mimosa bars and terrific food. I actually looked forward to going to those events, because the children would be entertained and I got to spend time with adult friends. Now, when we throw a party for our girls, we always make sure there's great food and time-appropriate adult beverages are present—so long as the magician, puppeteer, or juggler is entertaining the children!

Hacks for Perfectionists

LIFE HACK 100

Do not let perfectionism be the death of progress. This might be the most important hack of the entire book. À la the Pareto principle, if you can do 80 percent of the things you want to do with the time you have, then trust your instincts, go with your intuition, synthesize quickly, and go. The incremental 20 percent may simply yield diminishing returns.

Hacks for Snacks

LIFE HACK: POSTSCRIPT

Eat more quinoa. I always have a container of cooked quinoa in the fridge—it's my favorite healthy snack. It's tasty, nutritious, and easy to pop in a spoonful for a boost of energy on a busy day. Quinoa makes a perfect pairing with scrambled eggs in the morning or with grated cheese, vegetables, and a glass of wine as a light dinner. Sub-hack: make sure it isn't in your teeth before meetings. You're welcome.

And that's a (W)Rap(p)!

CONCLUSION: KEEP SWINGING

Before Hal became Husband Hal, he had a successful career as a major league baseball player. He was a first basemen with the Yankees, Kansas City Royals, and Detroit Tigers, and in 1990, he won a World Series championship with the Cincinnati Reds. After he retired, he became a professional scout for the Boston Red Sox and then a pro scouting director for the Los Angeles Angels. Years before we met, he made his debut on a Wheaties cereal box.

Suffice it to say, Hal knows a thing or two about baseball. So it's no surprise he instilled in me one of the greatest life lessons of all time: "Until it's the ninth inning and the third out, keep swinging."

Life will throw you no end of curveballs. That's what life does. Sometimes they're mundane: your car battery won't start, your child gets a head cold, your colleague misses an important meeting. These things are irritating and disruptive but relatively easily overcome. Other curveballs result in a far bigger impact—like when you lose a trusted executive at your company, or a childcare professional who has been with your family for years leaves a note on the kitchen counter to tell you she's quitting.

When the ball is spiraling toward you at breakneck pace, it's normal to feel stunned. You didn't see it coming. If you did, it wouldn't be a curveball (or perhaps a slider). The challenging part is to not be reactive when you're still in shock. To live in that uncertain place for a moment without letting it overtake you. To acknowledge the fear, thank it, and send it on its way. To take a deep breath—then pivot.

You can't avoid the curveballs. They will come at you in every area, every industry, every walk of life. I've faced them as a mom, wife, entrepreneur, executive, friend—you name it. But I don't run from them. I've learned to apply my brother Anthony Rapp's timeless advice: "The only way out is through."

The truth is, I love curveballs, because each one comes with a question: What the hell are you going to do about it?

My answer probably won't surprise you.

Keep swinging.

I've written love letters to my husband, my daughters, my brothers, and many dear friends and family over the years. This book of hacks is my love letter to *you*. It's a collection of all the strategies, shortcuts, and secrets I've accumulated as part of my lifelong commitment to keep swinging, whether it's in the businesses I've created or the relationships I've built.

I'll end with one of my favorite quotes by mountaineer, explorer, and philanthropist Edmund Hillary: "It is not the mountain we conquer, but ourselves. You don't have to be a fantastic hero to do certain things— to compete. You can be just an ordinary chap, sufficiently motivated to reach challenging goals. People do not decide to become extraordinary. They decide to accomplish extraordinary things."

May you accomplish a life of extraordinary things. And may this book of one hundred hacks for achieving your goals enable you to do so with greater efficiency and impact.

APPENDIX: READING LIST

Atlas Shrugged by Ayn Rand (Signet, 1996).

Becoming by Michelle Obama (Crown Publishing Group, 2018).

Fair Game by Valerie Plame Wilson (Simon & Schuster, 2008).

Finding My Voice by Valerie Jarrett (Viking, 2019).

From the Ground Up: A Journey to Reimagine the Promise of America by Howard Schultz (Random House, 2019).

Learning to Lead : The Journey to Leading Yourself, Leading Others, and Leading an Organization by Ron Williams with Karl Weber (Greenleaf Book Group Press, 2019).

My Life So Far by Jane Fonda (Random House, 2006).

Open: An Autobiography by Andre Agassi (Vintage, 2010).

The Algebra of Happiness by Scott Galloway (Portfolio, 2019).

The CEO Next Door: The 4 Behaviors that Transform Ordinary People into World-Class Leaders by Elena L. Botelho, Kim R. Powell, Tahl Raz (Currency, 2018).

The First 90 Days: Proven Strategies for Getting Up to Speed Faster and Smarter by Michael Watkins (Gildan Media, 2013).

The Jewelers Jeweler by Oscar Heyman, Yvonne Markowitz, Elizabeth Hamilton (MFA Publications, 2017).

You're in Charge, Now What?: The 8 Point Plan by Thomas J. Neff and James M. Citrin (Crown Business, 2007).

MORE FROM ALYSSA

To learn more about Alyssa and what she is up to, go to
www.alyssarapp.com.

Childhood Photos

Childhood Photo

Alyssa, Gymnastics Action Shot (1997)

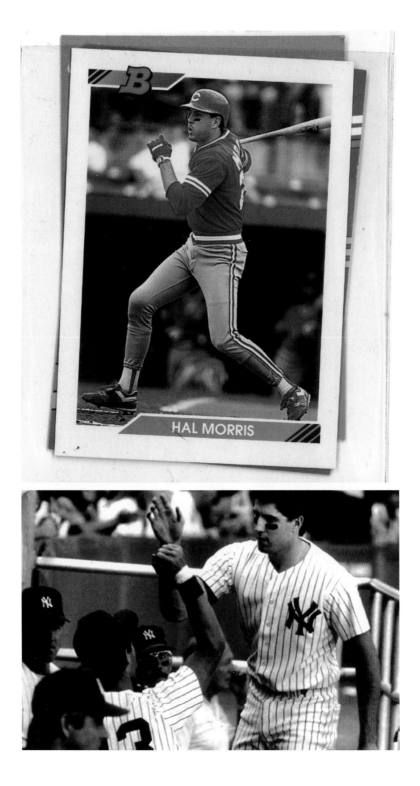

HAL MORRIS

Opposite, top: Hal's Baseball Card
Opposite, bottom: Hal Morris, NY Yankees
Above: Hal Morris, Cincinnati Reds

President Obama and Alyssa

Fmr. Ambassador Fay Hartog-Levin, Alyssa Rapp, Jeffrey Rapp, and Daniel
Levin at President Obama's 2012 Inauguration

Alyssa Rapp and Hal Morris, Wedding Photo

Top: Alyssa and Hal, Wedding Photo (2011)
Bottom: Alyssa and Jeff Rapp, Mt. Kilimanjaro

Top: Near Scarsdale, NY, visiting "Opa" (1998) with Cousins Jocelyn and Emery Stanton, Brother Jeff Rapp, Aunts Ellie Hartog and Anna DeLeeuw, and Mom Fay Hartog-Levin.
Bottom: Close Friends Bridget Alsdorf, Lisa Davis, Kate Douglas-Hamilton, Emily Melton, and Amanda Munoz with Alyssa in The Hague (2011) When Visiting the Fay Hartog-Levin Ambassadorial Residences for Alyssa's "Bachelorette" Experience

Baby Audrey, Hal, Alyssa (2011)

Audrey and Henriette Morris

Alyssa and Cofounder Kimberly Donaldson Receiving Two Empact 100
Showcase Awards as Entrepreneurs of Bottlenotes, on the Floor of
the United Nations

Top: Audrey and Henriette Morris
Bottom: From left to right, Ken Ithipol and Anthony Rapp ... at Jeff Rapp and
Amanda Kane's Wedding

Childhood Drawings